BOYS
WILL BE . . .?

Sex Education and Young Men

Neil Davidson

Bedford Square Press

Published by
BEDFORD SQUARE PRESS of the
National Council for Voluntary Organisations
26 Bedford Square, London WC1B 3HU

First published 1990

Typeset by BookEns, Saffron Walden, Essex
Printed and bound in Great Britain by J W Arrowsmith, Bristol
Cover printed by Heyford Press

British Library Cataloguing in Publication Data
Davidson, Neil
    Boys will be . . .? – (Survival handbooks).
    1. Man. Sexuality – Sociological perspectives
    I. Title   II. Series
306.7

ISBN 0-7199-1275-X

BOYS WILL BE . . .?

Neil Davidson comes from
a youth worker and has 10 ye.
young people in a variety of settin
has worked for New Grapevine, a sex
counselling project based in north Londo.
counselling young men. He has also worked
trainer, running courses on working with boys
with young men, and other issues concerning me

He has run courses for many organisations and
including the Family Planning Association, the Terren
Trust, the Institute of Education, the National Aidsline
social services departments.

He currently works as a trainer in sex and AIDS educati
for Save the Children.

Contents

Acknowledgements

Many thanks go to Trefor Lloyd (of Everyman Publications) who offered much encouragement and important criticism throughout the writing of this book. Sue Ryall and Alan Turkie read complete drafts, gave thoughtful feedback and were very supportive. Thank you. I owe you all a great deal. Others have given their time to read parts of the text and given back both enthusiasm and vital criticism. Many thanks to Ray Seabrook, Mark Webb and Frankie Lynch.

Thanks also go to Bill Mayblin for helping me build a picture of how the book should look.

Special thanks to Jacqui Stearn who not only read the text but picked me off the floor on many occasions, dusted me down and set me on my way again, listening to my doubts but never tolerating them. You are an inspiration – thank you.

There have been too many groups of young men I have worked with to thank individually, but obviously I couldn't have done it without them.

To Dave, Graeme, Bill, Colin, Duncan and Stuart who talked and listened with me when I was a young man.

What kind of book is this?

This is a book about men and sex. More specifically, it is about encouraging men, both young and adult, to start talking about sex. 'Do they ever do anything else?' I hear you cry. It's true that in public places – the youth club, the changing room, the pub, the golf club, the boardroom and behind the bike sheds – men talk about sex. But this talking is almost always about competition, banter, ridicule, boasting, rather than about communication or learning.

The main aim of this book, therefore, is to inspire confidence in *men* to start talking with young men and with each other, about what they really feel, think, and believe sex to be about. However, I hope that women who are working with young men may also find it useful, either directly as a resource in their own work or as background information, in supporting men in this area of work. It is aimed at youth workers, teachers, Intermediate Treatment workers, Employment Training Scheme supervisors, social workers – anyone who works with young men and is committed to the best in them, to young men as something more than 'problems'.

It is a 'how-to-get-started' book for those who maybe think that they 'don't know enough', 'don't know where to start' but do want to do something.

Part I starts with a chapter on 'Why sex education?' which looks at the context for sex education with young men in Britain today: AIDS, child sexual abuse, male violence and porn. How do these relate to the way men learn to be sexual, to the meaning we give to 'being a man'? What kind of sex education have we had? What kind of sex education do we need?

The chapter on 'Men and sex' gives some background to the process whereby men learn to be sexual. The next chapter contains the results of a survey of a cross-section of over sixty men who were asked about their experiences of growing up to be male and sexual. (The appendix includes some exercises for workers to help them relate to their own experiences around sex.)

A chapter on 'Working with young men' looks at running a sex education group with young men including planning, getting support and using resources.

Part II 'Sessions and resources' covers seven key areas which could be used to form the basis of a sex education group. A series of seven sessions with young men are described highlighting important issues and information to be looked at, problems that could arise, etc. This is followed by several recommended resource ideas which could be used to bring up the issue, e.g. exercises, videos, etc.

The book ends with a comprehensive list of sources of further information and other resources including games, films and videos, books, articles and useful organisations.

Part I
Before you start

1 Why sex education?

Sex is everywhere, or so it seems. It is a widespread, popular belief that sex is out in the open and has been so since the birth of the 'Permissive Society' back in the 1960s. Since then we have become more relaxed, open and tolerant. For some this is progress, for others it is evidence of a decline in moral values.

INTRO

Certainly there is much evidence to suggest that we have made some fairly significant shifts in our attitudes and behaviour in relation to sex. Legalised abortion, more accessible contraception, single-parent families, 'living together' outside marriage, and to a certain degree lesbian and gay sexuality, are all accepted (or at least tolerated) in a way unthinkable 25 years ago. Running parallel to this growth in more liberal attitudes to sex, however, is the way in which 'sex', in the shape of women's bodies, has become common currency in TV, films, newspapers, advertising and pop music. 'Sex' equals money and the commercial exploitation of women's bodies has become the norm.

Everybody is happily doing it, watching it, reading or talking about it. Or are they? Recent developments have done much to undermine this simplistic viewpoint:

- Obviously, the belated acknowledgement that AIDS is a threat to the *whole* population has had a profound effect on the way we feel and think about sex (even if this change has yet to clearly show itself in relation to our behaviour). Everybody's lives are now different, in some way because of it, and as the virus continues to spread then its affect on our lives will continue to deepen.
- The growing recognition of the scale of child sexual abuse has sent waves of horror, incomprehension, and disbelief

across the country. In a similar way to AIDS, the uncovering of sexual abuse has threatened some of our most basic 'common sense' assumptions.

- Like the abuse of children, violence, including sexual violence against women, is not new. Yet recently we have seen an upsurge in anger and outrage not only at the full scale and horror of the crimes, but also at the way in which they are dealt with.

- Closely linked with this are growing awareness and campaigns to deal with the damage done by pornography, not only through the increased availability of 'hardcore' porn but also in the popular press through 'Page 3'. Once the province of the pro-censorship lobby, porn has become a widespread public issue.

The cumulative effect ot these different 'problems' has lead to an atmosphere in which fear and confusion reign. Taken individually these issues can be successfully compartmentalised and thus avoid a deeper scrutiny. A superficial examination of these different issues seems to show no connection other than the fact that they are all, in some way, connected to sex. Yet if we look more closely two underlying patterns emerge.

The first is the fact that we find these problems so very hard to talk about. We seem to have neither an adequate language nor experience to deal with them in terms of anything other than horror, outrage, blaming or embarrassment. Most of us do not learn ways of dealing with the sexual difficulties that may arise in our lives. Our lack of ability to communicate to each other keeps us isolated and leaves us impotent, unable to conceive of change. To deal with this we need to learn to express and share our feelings, thoughts and values about sex with other people and to receive help and support when we need it. In short, we need comprehensive sex education to be available and accessible to all.

The second theme connecting these contemporary 'crises' is *men* and *sexuality*. If we look closely at these problems, it is possible to see that men's attitudes and behaviour are a common factor. It is heterosexual men's unwillingness to change sexual behaviour or to use condoms which is proving to be the most problematic aspect of the fight to prevent the spread of the HIV virus. Child sexual abuse is carried out almost exclusively by men. Violent assault and rape of women by men is increasing as is male violence on other men. The porn industry is run by and for men.

Therefore we also need a sex education which takes an

understanding of gender – how we learn to be men and women – as the context for learning about sex and sexuality.

But in recognising the superficiality of the view that there has been some kind of glorious 'sexual revolution', we should be careful not to forget one very important fact – sex can be wonderful. For anyone looking more closely at, or working with, issues of sex and relationships, it's very easy to see only what is difficult and problematic. And certainly, as I've suggested above there is plenty to be concerned about. But it is the potential that sex has for offering fulfillment, for giving us joy and pleasure and bringing us closer to people that makes this work so important. The kind of sex education we need is also one in which the life-enhancing qualities of sexual relationships are placed at the centre.

Learning about sex

Even if these current major problems did not exist then there would still be a need for a major re-evaluation of the way we approach learning about sex. What their existence does is to add a sense of urgency to the need for change in what has always been a major blind spot in our society. Learning about sex has largely been a haphazard, fearful, lonely or incomplete process. This has led to much unhappiness, inhibition, prejudice and frustration. That many people do find pleasure and happiness in their sexual lives is probably as much a result of good fortune as it is of conscious learning. Indeed, most of us tend to be so unused to clear and relaxed communication around sex that we find it as difficult and embarrassing to share the joy or excitement we do feel, as we do to talk about our problems.

Most of us have had very little help in learning about sex, tending rather to pick things us as we go along. Most parents, because of their own experiences find it difficult to talk to their children about sex. Consequently what learning there is takes place secretly, often guiltily. The so called 'sexual revolution' of the 1960s brought about the expectation, or even the appearance that we could all talk and learn about sex openly and honestly. Yet in reality we still huddle furtively, behind closed doors, talking about sex in whispers.

The pressures facing young people today are enormous. They have inherited not only traditions of secrecy and the liberalising effects of the 1960s, but also the increased exploitation of sex for profit. In addition to the contradictions this brings they are also having to grow into adulthood at a time when sex and sexual relationships are faced with new crises which threaten old certainties and assumptions.

There is pressure from friends or the media to be sexual, but what about AIDS? What also of the conflict between these influences and more 'traditional' values coming from family, culture or religion? What of the difficulties in reconciling pornographic images of women and real-life relationships? What models of male sexuality are young men given other than ones which present them as sexual predators? We too often expect young people to deal with these, and many other difficult issues around sex, on their own.

What kind of sex education?

Historically sex education has been about the 'facts of life' and that usually meant someone else's life – a frog's or a rabbit's. When the 'facts' were applied to human beings this was most often done in such a way as to fail to indicate that human sex was anything more than a mechanical process on a par with the workings of a steam engine. Surely this is a thing of the past? Yes and no. Certainly there is less coyness, and both parents and teachers take a much more direct and honest approach to human reproduction. Unfortunately 'sex' is often still missing. By sticking to 'the facts of life' we leave out the *desires*, *feelings*, *behaviours* and *opinions* which constitute the way we experience our sexuality. Only by including what we feel, do, think and believe will we be able to provide the means by which we can tackle our current problems. Fundamentally we need to encourage and support young people to be able to talk openly and honestly about sex. This means putting *communication* at the centre of the learning process, for by keeping young people quiet, isolated and ignorant we may be condemning them to unhappiness, unfulfillment, abuse, illness and death. It doesn't have to be this way.

Whose responsibility is it?

For most of us school is the only place we would have been likely to get any sex education. Although many young people do now receive sex education as part of their school education, it still forms a relatively small part of the overall curriculum, often appearing as a 'one-off' event. Much of the good work that has been done by teachers who have sought to integrate sex and sexuality into the wider context of pupils' personal and social development, is now under threat from recent government initiatives. Clause 28 and the Education Act 1986 threaten to close down the opportunities for developing sex education. Many school governors who now have this responsibility will undoubtedly opt for a sex education component in the curriculum, yet what kind of guidance and practical support will they receive in implementing such a programme?

Unfortunately there have been few people who have felt confident enough to offer such guidance and expertise. Adults, including parents and education professionals, were the children of yesterday who were themselves without adequate sex education. Currently there is still very little input in, for example, teacher or youth work training to cover the teaching of sex education.

So who *is* responsible? There is no time and certainly no need to leave sex education to the small number of 'experts'. In some way we *all* have a part to play. In one way or another, sex affects us all and given a degree of self-confidence those of us involved in young people's education and development can play an active part in their learning. I hope that this book will help play a part in boosting this self-confidence.

Sex education with young men

For a long time the burden of society's sexual problems has been carried by women. Such sex education as we have had has been carried out with the aim of helping keep young women 'out of trouble'. This is sex education as a form of damage limitation rather than a way of addressing young women's needs. Much of this approach to sex education has, however, changed in recent years, particularly in youth work where there has been a growing emphasis on work with young women which puts them and their needs first. This new emphasis has focused on looking at sex and sexuality and encouraging young women to regain control of this aspect of their lives. The impetus of this work has done much to challenge old notions of what youth work and sex education are about.

Traditionally, though, in terms of sex education, young men have been seen as too far beyond the pale to be worth bothering about, and until very recently there has been no comparable shift in our attitudes and work with young men. 'Boys will be boys' relfects a common belief that men are incapable of change, especially in relation to sex. This results in a similar 'damage limitation' approach to our current problems. If men cannot change, so the argument goes, then we must protect women and children from them by better 'policing' and more severe punishment. Inevitably this leaves many women feeling fearful, angry and frustrated and many men feeling confused, defensive or guilty.

In fact, men *can* change and this becomes possible if we begin to look at our current model of masculinity – what we understand being a man to be about – and see that it is this model that is at fault rather than the fact of being a man. Recently, more positive work with young men has developed which takes as a starting point an understanding of how men learn to be men and the limits this places on us. If we take this approach and apply it to sex education, then we come up with a realistic way of starting to tackle the serious problems we are currently facing about sex.

This kind of sex education can present young men with the opportunity to question the assumptions and stereotypes they carry about being men. By focusing on young men and their sexuality in a *positive* way, we can encourage them to break out of the cycle of oppressive behaviour that all too easily becomes habitual. It is a sex education which encourages the sharing of thoughts, feelings, and behaviours that would not normally be discussed, and through doing this with other men, it helps dissolve the isolation which glues men's 'unchangeableness' together.

2 Men and sex

Sex and gender

Boys are born male but they are not born men. This may seem
fairly obvious, but being male and being a 'man' often get
confused. The difference is important if we want to understand
and solve the problems that currently centre on men and their
sexuality.

Being male refers to our biological sex. If we look at two
newborn babies, the differences between male and female are,
biologically speaking, relatively superficial although it is obvious
that they do exist. The terms 'man' or 'woman' refer to our
gender and used precisely they apply to our behaviour,
attitudes and aptitudes rather than to anything physiological.

If we look again at our two newborn babies it will be pretty
hard to identify any gender differences. Babies, in terms of
behaviour, qualities, attributes, etc. are just . . . babies, doing
what babies do. Becoming a 'boy' or a 'girl' and later a 'man' or
a 'woman' is the result of a process of *learning*. This process
starts so early that attributes that are in fact learned are
commonly described as 'naturally' male or female. Before they
have even left hospital baby boys may already be being
described as 'loud', 'tough', 'a proper little man', etc. Similarly,
female babies may at this point already have embarked upon a
lifetime of being 'pretty in pink', 'soft', 'sweet', etc. Our gender
'training' starts as soon as we are born.

The precise form of this 'training' will of course vary
depending on a number of factors. Class, race, religion, culture
all make different kinds of men of us. A working class Catholic
young man will receive a different set of messages from a
middle class Jewish young man. Boys from a black, Afro-
Carribean culture will grow to be men influenced both by its

traditions and, of course by the racism they experience from
white society. Young Asian men will experience themselves
differently again as they too experience racism, but also may be
trying to deal with both the secular influences of mainstream
white society and the more 'traditional' values of Islam or
Hinduism. If we were to look wider afield, to non-European or
so-called 'primitive' societies, then they could provide us with
even more examples of the diversity of 'manhood' that exists.

Yet, although there are obviously many ways to 'be a man',
there are aspects of the experience which are, if not universal, at
least recognisably common to most men in Western
industrialised cultures.The two areas in which this seems most
obvious is in our attitudes to women and to our sexuality. In
working with men it is important to recognise and honour the
differences between us, but also to acknowledge what it is that
we have in common.

In the rest of this chapter I offer some of my thinking about
the process whereby boys become men and become sexual. It is
informed both by my own upbringing as a white, lower middle
class, Scottish man, and by my work with young white and
black (Afro Carribean) working class men in London. This is, of
course, a limited view. Nonetheless, I hope that it is still useful
as a way in to thinking both about ourselves and sexuality and
about the young men we work with.

Sexuality

Sexuality is commonly seen as a crucial part of the difference
between men and women, and it is the supposed 'natural'
differences in our sexualities that forms one of the central
pillars of our gender identity. But the extent to which men and
women actually are different sexually is a result not of different
'natures', or because a man has a penis and a woman a vagina,
but because we learn different things as we grow to be 'men'
and 'women'.

Becoming sexual and becoming a man are commonly held, at
least in secular Western societies, to be part of the same
process, one that happens as a result of physiological changes
we go through in puberty. Becoming 'sexual' is often rather
narrowly linked with both procreation and intercourse (from
which belief stems some of the prejudice against lesbian and
gay sexuality as 'abnormal').

However, if we widen 'sexuality' to include the enjoyment of
our own bodies, the need for physical affection, and closeness
with others, then it is fairly obvious that this starts much earlier.

In fact this need for *sensuality* starts just about as soon as we are born. Unfortunately many adults often find this hard to accept and try to limit the expression of these needs and desires. They do this by teaching us to be 'boys' in a process which not only represses our broad-based childhood sensuality but which builds the framework for the learning that will take place from puberty onwards when we are finally given the permission to be 'sexual'.

Little boy blue – birth to school age

Human babies are born delighting in their own sensuality and curious about their own bodies. Our earliest 'sexual' expression is the joy and excitement of our own physical-ness and the exploration of our immediate surroundings through our senses: touch, taste, sound and vision. Unfortunately, what happens in these first years is that adults try to control these tendencies, and our bodies. They may discourage us from touching ourselves (penises, vulvas and bums are particularly 'naughty'). This happens because most of us were brought up by parents whose *own* parents were uncomfortable dealing with sexuality, and so a cycle of sexuality as 'naughty' or wrong, as something to be hidden or feel guilty about gets perpetuated.

Much more openly, but still largely unconsciously, we are taught the rules about what being male means. In all sorts of ways, some explicit, some subtle, 'boys' are distinguished from 'girls' in terms of gender as well as biological sex. The 'naturalness' of such distinctions is taken for granted. Yet in practice the making of five-year-old boys from male babies requires time and energy on the part of the parents, adults and other children. The lesson that 'boys don't cry' is not easily learnt. By the age of five much of what is taken to be 'normal' male behaviour, attitudes and aptitudes has been formed. It is upon these foundations that a boy learns and relearns the lessons of what it means to be a man.

Boys' sexual development is intertwined with their learning about what 'boys' should be and do. The most obvious example of this process is the way in which as boys we learn to repress our sensuality and learn that sex is something to do specifically with our genitals. This may arise because boys are permitted to touch their genitals in order to pee and so may discover there is pleasure to be had there also, albeit secretly. Girls, on the other hand, are firmly discouraged from touching or even looking at themselves 'down there'. On a wider social level boys are encouraged to focus on activity, on achieving a 'result', on using their hands, on becoming 'capable' They are early on taught to 'get on with things', to make and do rather than communicate with others. Even the expression of pleasure or delight itself (squealing, giggling, being excited) is seen as 'girlish' and so frowned upon in boys.

Early gender messages

'Be a big boy and don't cry.'
'Be brave.'
'He's a proper little man.'
'He's very good with his hands – just like his Dad.'
'Eat your porridge or you won't grow up to be big and strong just like Daddy.'
'Don't be a cissy.'
'He's got to learn to stand on his own two feet.'

Early sexual messages

'Don't touch that, it's dirty.'
'I'll tell you all about it when we get home.'
'You mustn't say that, it's a very rude word.'
'Don't do that, it's not very nice, is it.'
'You'll find out when you're older.'
'That's private – you mustn't tell/show anyone.'

Slugs and snails – school age to puberty

As we get older, the influences our learning multiply rapidly. School, other children, television, books and comics all start to play an important part in both our learning about gender and about sex. The increased contact with the wider world outside the family helps to form our identity as we become more and more directly affected by factors of class, race, religion and culture.

This increased contact and our growing verbal intelligence mean that parents and other adults become even more active in enforcing 'rules' about what is acceptable behaviour and language. For some of us, silence and embarrassment from adults may be just as important as more direct intervention. We may learn by soaking up the 'atmosphere' around the issue of sex as much as by direct teaching. It's worth repeating here that parents, teachers and other adults are not doing this out of malevolence, but rather because this is what they learned themselves as children.

Many children do receive some formal sex education, yet

these carry little weight in comparison to the unconscious messages that get passed on. Sex is still something to be discussed in secret, giggled about, or used as a weapon to insult other children or to get back at adults. By the time a boy is 11 he will have learnt to 'set aside childish things': qualities like vulnerability, dependance, fear, gentleness, sensuality. In addition to giving up 'childish' qualities he may also have to give up girls as friends in order to be fully 'one of the boys'.

This is a time when being kissed by granny, crying when you skin your knee and being afraid of the dark start to be problematic. Of course, given that every little boy is used to feeling scared or vulnerable or in need of affection, it is very hard to set these feelings aside and no man ever is completely successful in doing so. What he does is to bury these feelings. For some this burying may be very deep, but others may experience real conflict between what they feel and desire inside and what they are publicly supposed to be. Different cultures will permit and forbid different feelings in boys. In some cultures, for example, showing fear may be forbidden but showing grief or sadness expected. In others, boys will be expected to bury everything except anger.

If you watch young boys up to the age of 11 you will see them trying on for size the behaviours and attitudes men are supposed to have. What this means in terms of sex is a phase of experimenting with swearing, verbally abusing other children, embarrassing adults with 'awkward' questions, giggling over some secret or bragging about what they know. Others may seem to have no interest in sex at all, preferring to plough their energy into football, train sets or whatever. In practice, many boys may fluctuate within these two tendencies, sometimes 'acting out' and at others being sullenly disinterested and solitary. Both kinds of behaviour are recognisably characteristic of many adult men's behaviour in general and towards sex in particular.

When does a boy become a man? Puberty to adulthood

Adolescence is popularly seen as a transition period: you enter as a child and at some unspecified time you emerge as an adult. Childhood and adulthood are seen as two distinct states of being. At its simplest level this distinction translates as adult = powerful, child = powerless. This understandably makes the transition period rather difficult. Unlike many other societies and religions, e.g. Judaism, Islam and many Third World cultures, mainstream Western secular cultures have no formal 'rites of passage' which could help to ease this process.

As children, boys gradually learned the qualities required of them as men in the making. Reaching adolescence makes it imperative that they adopt these qualities and finally let go of anything that is 'childish' or 'girlish'. In practice this rejection of parts of ourselves is both brutal and totally unrealistic. As a result as boys we become caught up in the need to *prove* that we are men. It is an impossible task because there are still times when we feel vulnerable, weak, confused, frightened, etc. and are unable to hide it. Proving becomes the norm until all the undesirable qualities are successfully removed which, of course, is never.

All this would be difficult enough in itself but the arrival of puberty makes it an even more traumatic time for many young men. Wet dreams, uncontrollable erections, rapid growth, increased sweat production can make life confusing and upsetting. What is worse is that as young men we are expected to go through these horrors on our own. To need support, to be confused or frightened would be to show that you are not really a man.

With the onset of puberty this task of 'becoming a man' becomes fused with the task of 'becoming sexual'. Puberty seems to allow the transformation of what were originally in early childhood *sensual* experiences into 'sexual' ones. That this period is seen as the emergence of proper adult sexuality may well be so because of the commonly accepted association of sex with reproduction: becoming biologically capable of fatherhood means having to accept the responsibility of becoming a man.

At this stage in our development sexuality becomes one of the main arenas in which we locate our identity as men. This does not mean that all young men are always and only interested in sex. But other people: parents, peers, teachers, the media, often expect this and identify us in terms of our (hetero)sexual activity, or lack of it. Unfortunately, though, most of the important elements that go into making a 'man' inhibit the process of learning about sex and it is this that is at the root of the crisis that currently surrounds men and sexuality.

Masculinity in crisis – men now

A major expectation of most models of masculinity is that adult men should be powerful. For all men this presents a problem, because there are always times when we do not experience ourselves to be so. Manhood means being part of a heirarchy,

where there are always winners and losers. Even for those at
the top there is no rest because someone is always waiting for
you to weaken so that they can take over. Sexism results from a
desire many men have to have *power over* others. Having power
over women may compensate for the ever present doubt about
being powerful enough in relation to other men. More
fundamentally, women (and children) have become, to men,
stereotyped symbols of powerlessness and as such are an ever-
present reminder to us of the part of *ourselves* that remains
weak and vulnerable in relation to others.

Of course, many of us resist this dominant view of
masculinity and because of cultural influences or individual
experiences find ways to be our own men. Up till now,
however, we have tended to do this in isolation,
accommodating ourselves to the dominant view in our public
lives even if we feel in private that we are different.

Sex itself may be used by heterosexual men as a means of
wielding power over women and of course, over children, too.
The damage this does is all too apparent: rape, violence, sexual
abuse, pornography. Even in so-called 'normal' relationships
between men and women, men often experience sex as a way
of feeling powerful and in control. Women become objects of
desire which men either use or must 'satisfy'. By turning sex
into a power struggle we lose the sense of our own sensuality,
of pleasure in ourselves as sexual beings and in doing so
become deeply estranged from ourselves.

But again sexuality and sexual relationships are an area of our
experience which is full of contradiction and conflict. On the
one hand, it is one of the most important arenas in which we
compete in an attempt to prove our manhood. Yet on the other
hand, it holds the potential to bring down the structure of
beliefs that holds together what we believe 'being a man' is all
about.

Because of their very nature, sexual relationships have always
held out the possibility of a closeness which contradicts the
fundamental isolation at the heart of many men's experience
and which brings to the surface a whole range of feelings which
are normally repressed. Some men react to this possibility by
becoming even more 'male', by macho, violent, aggressive
behaviour, through 'sex without responsibility', by using
pornography or prostitution. Some men have seen sexual
relationships as a *refuge* from the need to keep up the public
image of manhood, a place where they could be soft,
vulnerable, where they could let themselves be 'mothered'. This
is true both for heterosexual men who, as a consequence,

depend on relationships with women only for this 'refuge', but also for gay men who in their public life may be just as pressured by the competitive male world.

Our models of masculinity are always changing and adapting, yet at a deeper level they have remained constant for a long time. The inherent contradictions in our sexuality have remained without the overall structure falling. In recent years, however, other factors have contributed to these long-standing contradictions, and together they add up to a very real 'crisis' for our current model of masculinity.

Several recent developments have contributed to this growing crisis;

- Feminism and the changing place of women in society has undermined many of the basic assumptions men had about their relationships and the power they held. Women's demands both in the public and private worlds have led to fear and confusion amongst many men.

- The changing economic conditions, principally widespread unemployment and the decline of traditional skills, have called into question the 'breadwinner' role, particularly for working-class men. For black men the promises of a materialistic society have proved to be even emptier. They more than white men have been denied the traditional male identity as 'worker'. And there have been changes too for middle-class men with the rise of the 'go-for-it' culture and the consequent increase in stress-related diseases, alcoholism, and emotional and relationship breakdown.

- The increased public profile of gay sexuality fundamentally threatens traditional models of masculinity and in particular men's isolation from each other. It is a visible symbol that men can be close. Gay sexuality also suggests the possibility of a very different kind of power relationship between men (even if in practice this may not always be the case).

- The increased attention given to child sex abuse has gradually meant a widespread questioning of men and their sexuality.

- The arrival of AIDS has directly challenged mens' sexuality. If men, gay as well as straight, are to survive, then part of what is required is the relinquishing of some traditional male sexual behaviour – casual anonymous sex, lack of communication, penetration as the only 'true' sex, a distaste for condoms. Significantly, it is gay men who seem far more able to adapt and change their ideas of what is appropriate sexual behaviour who are in the forefront of stopping the spread of the virus. The majority of heterosexual men still cling to 'the old ways'.

Men changing – where now for male sexuality?

That our models of being a man and of our sexuality are in crisis also means that there is now an opportunity for change. Because our 'manhood' and our sexuality are *learned*, then it is possible for us to assist this process of change. This is not the same as the creation of the 'New Man' much favoured by the glossy magazines, but rather the re-claiming of a man who is *already there* but hidden. Such a change is possible only if two basic assumptions about being a man (in particular a heterosexual man) are challenged. These are firstly that men should not, indeed cannot, show their feelings and secondly that we are independent and don't need closeness with others.

We need to be encouraged to acknowledge and express how we *feel* rather than just what we think. Sharing how we feel does of course take practice and at first this may seem threatening, but given the right kind of supportive atmosphere it can be done. Secondly we need to start to break down the barriers between ourselves and others and in particular between ourselves and other men. It is important to remember that this change is not about creating something new, but rather about remembering aspects of ourselves we have buried. Most men have had some experience of closeness, of expressing feelings, of sensuality, but these tend to get buried and forgotten about. We need to be encouraged to reclaim them. Talking about sex is a good place to start.

3 Growing up male, growing up sexual: a survey

Questionnaire – men learning about sex

Quoted below are 'edited highlights' from a questionnaire I sent out to a cross-section of about 60 men, black, white, working class, middle class, gay, straight, and from a variety of religious backgrounds. The questionnaire was answered anonymously. It was aimed at illustrating the experiences men have in growing up to be sexual. You might like to try answering it yourself as part of your own preparation or in a support group. It is not intended for use with groups of young men.

1 What is your earliest sensual/sexual memory?

'At age 8 having a sort of "coming" sensation on a climbing frame in the playground. It was very nice!'

'Kissing a class-mate's willy when I was 6 up the hills at the back of our house.'

'Secretly watching my aunt and uncle screwing.'

'Pre-school age, hanging around a large vibrating washing machine, watching my mother wash the family's underwear.'

'Sliding against my younger brother's body in the bath, aged 6.'

'Women's underwear, and what it must be like to touch women in it.'

'Probably an erection on the bus – all those vibrations!'

2 What was your first sexual experience with another person as an adolescent? Was it positive, exciting, frightening?

'Petting at a party with a girl. Exciting because it was fairly public and therefore recognised as my "coming of age".'

'About 14, kissing a girl at a New Year's Eve dance at midnight. Exciting and frightening. I didn't want to have to wait until next New Year's Eve to kiss a girl again!'

'Early teenage experience was with girls, a romanticised tingly closeness which had nothing to do with genitals. This was positive but did not in any way prepare me for the feelings I would have for other men as sexual partners.'

'My friend and I used to give each other blow-jobs.'

'Groping at parties under the influence of cider. It was exciting but the first time clothes were removed I remember feeling terrible guilt the next morning on my paper round. But it was a Sunday and on Monday at school guilt gave way to pride, of course.'

'Kissing behind a post office in the Alps.'

'The first experience was definitely more frightening than anything else. Was it even sexual? I went to the woods with a girl. All I remember was that she was wearing a padded bra, we groped in the caves, little talk but both desperate.'

3 What has been the most difficult aspect of learning to be a man sexually?

'To come to terms with being gay and being committed to a long-term relationship that is not monogamous.'

'I always fell in love with every girl I kissed.'

'Seeing myself positively as a sexual person has been hard, because of my self-control as a child. Masturbation became a secret, a 'behind the bathroom door' affair, where my erotic fantasies were always of men. Actually accepting my homosexual desire was *very* difficult and tied up with a general low self-esteem. It has taken some time to think about what I really want sexually and to feel good about me as an active sexual person – and also to feel OK about declining sexual contacts I don't want.'

'Trying to equate fantasy and reality, i.e. being happy about exploring mine and others' fantasies.'

'Maintaining a positive attitude towards my own sexuality whilst trying to understand how it oppresses women. Rebuilding on a sounder foundation – it takes a long time.'

'Learning not to be ashamed of myself, my body, my needs, my desires.'

'Keeping sexism out of sex.'

'Most difficult has been the isolation and not really knowing where sex fits in my life. All the bravado didn't really leave any scope for finding out.'

4 What was your happiest/funniest/most exciting memory of learning to be a man sexually?

'Most exciting was realising that I didn't have to do it if I didn't want to. Separating "lustful" from "sexual". This has released me from having to think about it so much.'

'Going camping with two other boys, aged 14, the three of us running around a lake calling out the names of the buxom girls we imagined we were in love with.'

'My most exciting memory of learning to be a man sexually was the last time I was in bed with someone, because I always remember that better than anything before. One of my most exciting experiences was getting to know about guiltless sex again after years of doubt around being "anti-sexist" in bed. Learning to feel that my needs and desires could be expressed and enjoyed as much as catering to my partners.'

'Definitely being seduced by two older women, when I was 16. They were drunk and uninhibited, I was athletic. I learned and experienced a lot in one afternoon. It was great!'

'Meeting another's gaze knowingly, especially in a crowd – that sexual bond. The underground during rush hour has had its advantages on at least two occasions!'

'The first time I had intercourse I wore two condoms for extra safety!'

'Coming out as a gay man and discovering sexual passion.'

5 Did you have any 'formal' sex education from parents, teachers etc.? What was this like?

'Yes, fairly good in that I was given the message that it was OK to be sexual.'

'No!'

'None that prepared me for the complexities of male sexuality as I experience them. I am still angry about that.'

'A booklet from my parents.'

'We learned about horses and rabbits. It was very confusing.'

'From teachers we got a little practical contraceptive, VD advice but no emotional/sexual guidance. It was mostly non-existent, mostly crap.'

'My father gave me a book called *Boys and Sex*. It was useful.'

'We had a terrible sex talk at school about how evil it was to touch yourself or other boys.'

'No. Going to an all boys' school I think they thought any talk of sex would make us turn on each other. The quiet end of the sixties!'

6 Can you talk to other men about sex now? If so, under what circumstances, and what kind of talking?

'Yes. But I don't a lot. To be honest I'm not desperately interested in sex. I think closeness, intimacy and softness are more interesting and sex is lovely within these.'

'Yes. To friends in therapy, in a men's group, though some areas are always difficult.'

'Yes, fairly easily particularly with friends about feelings, experiences, desires.'

'I always have really. I've got a twin brother and we've always been close and been able to be honest and helpful with each other.'

'Professionally I spend a lot of time talking to young men about sex. In my private life the opportunity or need seldom arises. On the odd ocassion which it does it is very factual – no emotion, no embellishment, no fun.'

'With male friends, mostly gay, I can talk in a clinical and impersonal way about sex. It's probably hardest with my regular partner with whom I allow myself to be most vulnerable, because it brings up the issue of sex with other people and of my being a sexual person myself which has been difficult for me to embrace.'

'With close friends in a male sort of environment, e.g. having a pint in the pub.'

7. Do you have memories of talking about sex with other men as an adolescent?

'Only in the formal setting of sex education or by boasting about my/their sexual performances.

'Mostly in boasting or bragging at school.'

'As a child I talked mainly with girls about 'sex' focused on breasts and their mothers'/sisters' pubic hair! I *never* talked about sex with other men as an adolescent as far as I can remember. I didn't join in the sex talk that did abound at school. I was the controlled, 'good', non-sexual one.'

'Yes. And I think all of it was bullshit!'

'We didn't talk much and I remember real feelings of guilt after mutual masturbating sessions.'

'Yes, but mostly on the level of how far you got and what it was like when you got there.'

'Only the bravado, nudge, nudge stuff. No real talking, except maybe with my best mate.'

8 What do you think are the most important influences on you growing up to be a sexual man, e.g. from your religious, cultural, racial, class background? What kind of sexual man were you supposed to be?

'I was supposed to be soft and considerate, thoughtful, and think about the other person always.'

'Class. I was supposed to be tough, not scared. Go out and get 'em.'

'To be Jewish, middle class of my generation defined a kind of impotent, thwarted, agonised lustfulness (Portnoy!).'

'Anti-gay pressures from church and society in general and a lack of positive role models.'

'Strange religious preoccupations – I was brought up by Plymouth Bretheren. School determined a lot – ignorant playground bragging and glances at 'men only' magazines. In fact the only things I read that referred to sex explicitly were pornographic magazines or bizarre rabid Christian publications. Very helpful.'

'My class background says I should be straight and sometimes my political and cultural background wishes I was gay. The result is that I am sometimes a grudgingly heterosexual man.'

'I was "supposed" to be an exclusively heterosexual, married middle-class Catholic. It has been acknowledged since that my father abused my sister and that my parents' relationship (including sexual) was not good, to say the least. Probably more than anything this has affected my life, making it hard to see male sexuality as something positive.'

'My family. Whilst I was taught to pursue a fulfilling sex life by my parents, there was an expectation to be straight and have kids. As a gay man my peers have been the biggest influence..'

9 If you are heterosexual have you had experiences of talking to gay men about sex? If you are gay what are your experiences in talking to heterosexual men about sex?

'Mainly in formal settings and they've been OK. Also with a few very close straight male friends but then often feeling like I have to explain myself and feeling inhibited about being very explicit in case I shock.'

'Hardly at all although I talked to a lesbian woman at college about her feelings.'

'I don't have a lot of intimate straight friends; when I do talk of sex I'm sure I'm quite smug, now that I recognise what a shitty thing heterosexual assumptions are. But I've also been pleasantly surprised by some men who have also challenged this and understand their sexuality rather than take it for granted. The sensual side is harder to talk to straight men about for me. There seems to be an unwritten rule which says "don't touch that level of feeling in me".'

'I thought about this for a while. I have only rarely talked to gay men about sex and then only in a professional capacity.'

'When we do [heterosexual] men are often surprised to talk frankly and are usually fairly guarded.'

'Yes. I have often found myself listening to gay men, rather than talking with them. Mainly because of the negative view there is of gay sex.'

10 Are you happy with the sexual aspects of your life at present? If so, what is good about it? If not, what would you like to be different?

'I feel I'm in transition. I am enjoying being close with people which usually means I don't feel sexual towards them. I don't really know what sex means to me. I think as my isolation from others continues to reduce, then so will the "turn-ons" as I have known them. That may mean sex becomes less of an issue in my life.'

'Yes I am but I'm often too tired to do it as often as I and my partner would like.'

'Yes. I'm married, monogomous, much loved, and there's sharing and fullness much of the time.'

'I would like a lover who I have a fairly rampant sex life with.'

'Yes but not always. What's good is that I'm sexually involved with people at the moment which is fun and exciting. Also as the result of one particularly honest and open sexual relationship I feel positive about myself again.'

'I'm beginning to enjoy safer sex!'

'My heterosexual hang-ups are under control, I enjoy myself, I think my partners enjoy themselves too. (That sounds as if I have hundreds, which of course, I do not.)'

'Not being committed to one person.'

'I'm exploring sex with people other than my regular partner. This is challenging our relationship in a good way and we both have external support. I suppose I'm only now beginning to work out what I like, and am like, being sexual.'

'Being married seven years, sex doesn't have the excitement it used to have. I see many women I fancy, although I probably couldn't cope with the guilt of an affair because the marriage is very happy.'

'Yes. I don't feel confined by the relationship I'm in. I feel like I'm still exploring my sexuality whilst getting a lot of physical and emotional enjoyment.'

4 Working with young men

Aims and motivation

Hopefully you have already decided to do some work with
young men around sex and are raring to get started, but before
you do, it's worth taking a little time to ask a few questions to
clarify *where* you want to go and *why*. Doing this helps avoid
the trap of setting ourselves unrealistic targets. In this way we
can channel our enthusiasm appropriately, retain and build on
our confidence and if we do encounter difficulties then we will
be able to keep them in perspective. This means asking some
questons both about the young men you are going to work with
and about yourself. It might be useful to keep these questions
and your answers to hand as a reference point as your work
progresses.

(If you haven't done work focusing specifically on young men
before it might be useful to have a look at Trefor Lloyd's book,
Work with Boys, which forms an excellent starting point for
anyone approaching work with young men from a perspective
of understanding masculinity (see Further information).

The young men

- What are the main issues/concerns about sex and sexuality
  for the young men you know?
- How does their unsureness about being a man affect their
  sexuality? What do they find most difficult about sex and
  relationships?
- What do you notice about the way young men talk about
  sex? Are there differences when they are talking amongst
  themselves, with young women around, with adults around,
  one to one?
- What differences do you notice about attitudes, behaviour,

values, language about sex across groupings of age, class, race and religion?

- Are you making any assumptions about the way young men feel, behave, and think about sex? Are they all heterosexual? Are they all sexually active?
- Does your current relationship with these young men include talking about sex?
- What do you like about the way the young men deal with sexual matters/their sexuality? What is positive about it?
- If you are going to do some work on sex, what activity/situation would be best: group work, informal work, counselling?

Yourself

- Why is work around sex important for you?
- Have you done any thinking about your own sexuality/sexual life? (Have you tried the questionnaire on pages 18–25?)
- How do you feel about talking to others about sexual matters?
- How do you feel about talking to others about your feelings?
- What makes you a good person to do this kind of work?
- What aspects of the work are you unsure of?
- What kind of support can you get for yourself?
- Are there any areas of your own sexuality/sexual life you don't feel prepared to discuss? Have you thought about why this is? How could you deal with these areas when they come up?

Developing a strategy

Having thought about these kind of questions we are now in a better position to develop an appropriate strategy for our work with young men. This means looking at ways to work which will best suit our aims, our own motivation, our particular skills and experience and the setting we work in. Work around sex and sexuality can happen anywhere. It can be done with groups or with individuals, or centred around one particular issue or many. Ideally it should be integrated into our everyday work with young people so that it becomes part and parcel of what good youth work, or teaching, is about.

However, we have to start somewhere. Most of the rest of this book is devoted to work with sex and sexuality in small groups. Running a group which specifically focuses on these issues is a good way to introduce them to young men who may never before have had the opportunity to discuss them. Working informally in groups and with individuals can (and indeed should) continue successfully on the impetus provided by such a group. A six- to eight-week group is not, of course, going to answer all the questions or resolve all the issues young men may have about sex or being men, so it is best not to see it in isolation from a wider commitment to, and strategy for, working with them.

Running a group

What kind of group?

The main aim for a sex education group is to raise awareness of the issues. It is a starting point for young men who have had little, if any, opportunity to talk about sex in a positive, 'safe' environment. It aims to allow young men to acknowledge and begin to express the ideas, feelings, attitudes and values they have about sex and sexuality. The characteristics of the kind of group I have in mind are that it is discussion based rather than 'therapeutic', short-term (six to eight weeks) rather than long term, and small (say no more that eight members who stay constant for the duration).

The first two characteristics are appropriate because I am aiming to describe a 'starter' group. Once individuals are used to the idea of a 'group' and of sharing experiences, then perhaps something that goes a bit deeper, for example, that looks more closely at feelings, might be appropriate. A relatively short time span also seems right, particularly since young men are so unused to sitting in groups 'just talking'. A set time span also gives you, the group leader, the chance to review the work, acknowledge achievements and stay fresh.

Any group with more than eight members tends to inhibit the free-flow of discussion and with young men encourages the emergence of a 'gang' identity where conformity is essential. As numbers get bigger, talking about sex becomes increasingly impersonal and decreases the likelihood of anyone offering a viewpoint which differs from traditional male stereotypes.

What age groups should I work with? All of them if possible, but not all together. Boys and young men seem to fall into their own natural groupings and I have found it best to stick to these when running groups and not try to mix too broad an age range.

The key issue in forming a group is *safety*. The best group is one in which the individuals involved feel safe, particularly in discussing something like sex. When at all possible let the group form naturally with young men choosing who they want to be with. If you are going to select the group then you need to think carefully about this issue. In what groupings are individuals most likely to open up and learn? You might want to run a group for young black Afro-Carribean men or young Asian men or young gay men. Don't, however, spend so much time agonising over the degree of safety that you end up doing nothing at all. The safer you make it, the better it will be, but it's bound to feel a bit risky to begin with, so dive in.

Race, culture, religion and class

Running a sex education group needs an understanding of the way in which factors of race, culture, religion and class affect the way we learn to be sexual. These factors also affect the way we learn to talk and communicate about sex, too. This means, particularly for white workers, that we should not make assumptions about what is acceptable, 'normal' or 'natural' in sex and be willing to look outside our own particular cultural experience. You may need to do some homework on the experience of any other racial, cultural, religious or class group you are unfamiliar with. For example, as a white worker I need to take some responsibility about finding out about young black men's experience by asking them what they feel, think and believe about sex and relationships. Even within the different black communities or cultures different people will hold different views. Young black men may have as widely differing views from each other as young white men. All young men are individuals – treat them as such.

A major part of working with young men around sex and sexuality is about looking at ways of helping them find alternatives to aspects of their lives where they are cast in oppressive roles. But it must also include a perspective on the ways in which *they themselves experience oppression*, both as young people and through racism and other forms of prejudice. We need to consider the effect this has on their sense of self in their day-to-day lives. Young people in general experience a sense of powerlessness in relation to adults. Their opinions, their needs and wishes are often not valued by adults. They are often subject to regular emotional and physical abuse from adults. We do not live in a society which, in practice, genuinely respects young people. For young black men this is compounded by racism, for young gay men by heterosexism and homophobia, for working class young men by classism.

Furthermore, the differences in beliefs, values, morals and traditions that get raised in looking at sexuality can all get used as ammunition for fear and prejudice by white against black, Christian against Muslim, Protestant against Catholic, heterosexual against gay and lesbian, etc. As a group leader you have an important role in interrupting this process.

What kind of 'groupwork'?

Most youth workers, teachers, Intermediate Treatment and Employment Training supervisors will already have the skills and experience to run a sex education group. What people often lack is *confidence*. This is because most of us have had little opportunity to talk about sex with other men in a positive environment. In the rest of this chapter I shall encourage you to use the skills you *already* have and making some suggestions which can help you to apply these to sex education.

Giving information

Good, clear, accurate information is a crucial part of learning about sex. Traditionally, sex education has focused almost exclusively on 'the facts of life', and although this approach is too limited, the 'facts' obviously do have their place. This doesn't mean that, as group leaders, we have to have all the answers at our fingertips, even though this is the kind of thing we, as men, have been taught to try and do. A certain amount of homework familiarising yourself with some key information and terms could, on the other hand, be useful.

Don't worry if you are asked a question you can't answer. Having access to information is just as important. It might be good for young men to witness a man prepared to say, 'I don't know everything there is to know about sex.' What is important is to respect young men's intelligence, curiosity and eagerness to learn.

Giving good, clear, accurate information is also an important way to tackle racism and other forms of prejudice. Sexual myths about gay men, black men, Asian men are common.

Creating the right environment

Young men want to talk about sex. They want to find out, to ask questions, to hear what others have to say, to say what they think and believe. Unfortunately, the way we are taught to be men does not encourage this. In particular, it does not encourage an attitude of mutual and shared co-operation.

Instead, we learn to score points with our ideas, to defend our values, to attack others' positions, to shout louder than anyone else, not to share our feelings with other men. All of this means that a sex education group can be strange, unfamiliar and frightening for young men. It means that young men can be at the same time both excited and enthusiastic about talking about sex, yet embarrassed and defensive, too. Creating an environment in which young men can learn, share and feel safe talking with other men about sex is the key to the work. But how do we do this?

By making the group 'special', a bit of an event, we let the young men know that their sexuality is worth taking seriously. This can be done by giving the group a good build-up, by 'selling' the idea well. Simple things, like providing comfortable chairs and a quiet room, can make a lot of difference to the start of a group in particular.

Setting 'ground rules' is an important part of the first session. By having a 'no banter, no put-downs' rule, for example, we designate this space as different from the everyday. Banter is one of the best tools men have for keeping themselves apart and isolated from each other. Similarly, by encouraging respect for what others say and affirming that nobody has to reveal anything they don't want to, we let the young men know that this is a 'special' place.

Obviously you need to use your discrimination about this. Too many rules rigidly applied will serve only to reinforce the young men's defensiveness and use up all your energy in trying to enforce them. A few simple 'ground rules' help to set boundaries and encourage young men to open up.

You may feel that some kinds of remark (such as racist, sexist, heterosexist) are out of order and need to be banned outright. This certainly lets young people know where you stand. Even more important is your responsibility to protect young black men or gay men, for example, from abuse. There may be times when you might want to challenge such attitudes and remarks as they come up, encouraging young men to explore what they are about, why they use them, what effect they have on others. A discussion about racism or anti-gay prejudice, however, should not be done at the expense of young black or gay men in the group.

Young men look to older men, brothers, fathers, footballers, pop stars, etc, as models of how to be men. Inevitably some of the time we ourselves may be fulfilling this role. The message we give out when talking about sex can have a big impact on the way the group operates. What kind of man do you come across as? Consider what aspects of yourself, what qualities, you are willing to show, and what effect this could have. Are you willing to reveal those parts of yourself which fall outside traditional notions of how men should, feel, act and think?

Given the rare opportunities men have to talk seriously about sex with other men, the way you behave in the groups is at least as important as the content of what you talk about. It is important, however, not to become paralysed by this process but rather to be aware of it. Everybody has their own unique and individual way of working and we all have strengths and limitations. Being self-conscious about always getting it right or trying to be 'anti-sexist man of the year' will be self-defeating.

Just as some young men will find themselves identifying with you, others will not. Obviously we are limited by our individual experience, by race, by our cultural, class and religious background. If we have the option then our choice of co-worker can help to offset this. It is, for example, obviously useful if you are working with black and white young men to have black and white group leaders.

Creating relationships

The relationships that develop between us and the young men and between the young men themselves are at the heart of the work. It is by paying attention to the quality of these relationships that learning about sex become possible.

If, as I have talked about earlier, growing up male and sexual means being competitive/frightened/defensive/isolated, then what we need to do in our relationships with young men is offer alternatives to these. We can do this in a number of ways:

- by showing a genuine interest in all the young men as individuals and to the traditions and cultures from which they come
- by approaching them with an attitude of respect for them as men
- by appreciating their contribution to the group, particularly if they show courage by expressing attitudes or feelings which go against the accepted 'norms' for men
- by challenging assumptions, stereotypes and prejudices that may be held, in a way which allows scope for change (i.e. challenge the attitudes or behaviour while respecting the person)
- by doing all of the above in relation to ourselves and our co-workers

- by being willing to be as honest as we can about ourselves
- by ensuring that a wide range of ideas, values and opinions gets heard in the group

A sense of humour

As we all know, sex can be a very serious business and a light touch is important in putting people at their ease. However, the nervous laughter and giggling which often accompanies discussions about sex are also a very good way of releasing the fear and embarrassment we have learned, so if you've got a sense of humour use it, and if you don't – develop one.

Preparation

Personal preparation

The most important thing is to do a bit of thinking and reflecting and if you've answered the questions in the section 'aims and motivation' then you are well on your way. Having done this you might also like to do some reading to brush up on the 'facts', although as I've emphasised earlier this doesn't mean ploughing your way through a medical dictionary. Most of the factual information you should need will be covered in 'Make It happy' (see 'Further information') and I would strongly recommend looking through this. If you are working with a colleague then obviously you will need time in discussion with them (see 'Support', page 40).

People preparation

There are a number of people you might want to talk to before running a group:

- You will need to approach the young men you want to work with to see if they are interested. This might involve some selling of the idea, unless of course they have already approached you. The idea of an all-male group getting together to talk about sex might be a little threatening for some of them.
- In the current climate, in particular, sex education is sometimes seen as a 'controversial' issue. Although there is no legal obligation to get consent, if the group consists of under-16s then it might be wise to discuss or send a letter about what you are planning with parents and get their

support. Recent studies have shown that most parents would be only too happy to have sex education done by someone else, such as a teacher, youth worker, etc. However, the passing of Clause 28 of the Local Government Bill (1988) highlights the extent of the fears some people still have about these issues.

• Find out if your LEA youth service, school or management committee has a policy on sex education. (If they don't you might want to get involved encouraging them to do so.) You may feel you want to get your youth officer's, head teacher's or manager's support. But don't get yourself bogged down in trying to get everybody's approval or permission.

• Other users of your club, centre or school may also need to know what you are planning. This could be important both as a way of dealing with any ill-feeling, resentment or disruption about the group, and more positively as a way of making a statement that sex education is on the agenda. You may find that the prospect of one group getting this kind of 'special treatment' builds up demand and you may have to consider some kind of rolling programme.

• Getting the support of your colleagues is just as vital. Some people may be suspicious, fearful or disapproving of this kind of work. Most adults will have had even less opportunity to discuss sexual matters in a safe, constructive way than young people. Although I don't believe that a sex education group needs much in the way of resources ploughed into it, it is, relatively speaking, a labour-intensive way of working. Even if your colleagues are already supportive of you, you may have to give up something else to do this work. This needs to be clearly agreed with those with whom you are working closely. In addition, these colleagues may well find themselves under extra pressure to deal with anyone who having been excluded from the group decides to register their protest by banging on doors, shouting obscenities and generally giving the other workers a hard time. If you have their support, then this kind of thing can be anticipated or avoided altogether. The best way to get this support is by being clear, open and enthusiastic about what you are doing.

Practical preparation

Having a comfortable, quiet room away from other activities will help reinforce the 'special' feel of the group. If you are working in a youth club, then it's a good idea to have the group as far away as possible from the main activities, thus minimising interruptions. It's also a good idea to avoid running the group when it might clash with a football match, a pool tournament, a trip out or 'Eastenders'.

Advance publicity in the form of posters and personal invitations are also crucial. You may need to remind participants several times in order to get through the 'take it or leave it' attitude some young men learn to adopt.

Planning

Setting the agenda – their issues and yours

You've identified your group, thought through how you're going to work with them, prepared your colleagues, found a room . . . now *what* exactly are you going to do with them?

Planning ahead, in the sense of being prepared to deal with a range of topics, is important. However, the degree of *detail* of this planning depends on how you work best. If you are very confident about dealing with a range of subjects, then you could let the agenda be determined by the young men at each session. On the other hand, perhaps you might feel you need a very tight structure, plenty of resources and the sessions planned weeks in advance. In practice most of us fall somewhere between the two.

An agenda for the group is likely to evolve as a result of both what the young men bring up and what you think the group should look at. My own experience is that if I ask a group what they want to do next week I'll be met with a resounding silence. During a session, however, someone may bring up something that grabs the group's interest and we discuss that rather than the prepared topic. How flexible you are with the content of the discussion is a matter for your discrimination. Keeping your basic aims fresh in your mind will help you decide. This might mean feeling frustrated that the hours spent swotting up on the finer points of anatomy have been wasted because the group preferred to talk about porn. Don't worry – your efforts will stand you in good stead at a later date.

Although planning is important it can lead to the trap of trying to have everything covered, trying to prepare yourself for every possible eventuality. As you gain experience in talking about the range of issues to do with sex you will find it much easier to be flexible. But this means taking a few risks, trying a few things out. While you are doing this it is worth remembering that the fact that you are running this group at all, that you are paying attention to these young men's sexuality is something they are unlikely to have experienced before and therefore is of enormous value in itself.

A sex education curriculum

Below I have set our a 'core' curriculum of sessions which I use as a starting point with every group I work with. Because of the unfamiliarity of the experience for most young men I tend to start a group by looking at some of the more factually based 'traditional' sex education subjects like anatomy, contraception, sexually transmitted diseases (STDs). Starting with these more familiar topics helps to 'break the ice' and get the group used to the idea that it's OK to talk seriously about sex. This helps to pave the way for dealing with topics that are more immediately threatening, like 'sexism' or 'being a man'. Of course, none of these 'factual' subjects are purely that. Contraception, for example, does require a factual input of what, where and how. It also includes questions about values – 'Who is responsible?', and of feelings – 'What is it like trying to buy condoms from a chemist?', and of attitudes – 'What do you think about a pill for men?' In the end, of course, it's up to you. Experiment. Try things out. Find out what works best for you and the young men you are working with.

A sample programme

Week 1 Introduction

Week 2 Bodies (anatomy, sexual response, etc.)

Week 3 Contraception

Week 4 AIDS/HIV and other sexually transmitted diseases (STDs)

Week 5 What is sexuality?

Week 6 Sexism – men and women

Week 7 Being a man

This programme forms the basis of the 'Sessions and resources' chapter that forms Part II of the book.

Setting a timescale

How long the group runs depends on you and the young men, but it is important with this kind of work to set a *fixed* number of sessions. This is so for two reasons:

- It contributes to making the group something 'special', and this is important in encouraging different behaviours and attitudes from the young men.
- It gives you and your co-workers the chance to evaluate and assess how the work has gone. By setting a timescale you check out how far you have achieved your aims.

This doesn't, of course, stop you from running a second series or from setting up other groups.

Evaluation

How do you know whether you are achieving your aims? Are the young men learning anything? What is happening in the group? Evaluation is the process whereby you answer questions like these. It is important for a number of reasons. It helps you assess how effective you are being, whether you are actually meeting your aims. It allows you to look at how well you are working and thus develop and improve your skills. It provides you with something concrete to show managers, funders, parents, something which we can use to justify continued support and funding. You may find that some people are suspicious of what you are doing. Evidence from evaluation can help allay fears and show the importance of the work.

Evaluating your work can appear to be a daunting task and it often seems like all we have time for is the work itself. But it doesn't have to take the form of a massive academic study. In fact, evaluation is something we all do anyway, even if it is only in the form of chatting with a colleague or listening to someone's casual comments at the end of an evening. However, with work like this, which is relatively new, it is important to try and do something more formal.

One aspect of this process involves asking yourself questions about what you feel and think about the work and whether you are meeting your original aims. You can do this in a number of ways: as part of regular 'de-briefing' with a co-worker after each session and also at the end of a series of sessions. Supervision or a support group are also places where you can not only 'off-load' your feelings about the work but also get support in checking how far you are meeting your aims. Talking with others also helps us look at how your skills are developing (see 'Support' on page 40).

Making notes of sessions, however brief, is a good way of keeping track. Try writing down what you saw happening as well as what you felt about a session. Perhaps recording what you did, who spoke the most, what issues were most enthusiastically discussed, any difficult moments, what the relationships were like. When it comes time to review the session it may be that patterns and issues emerge from which you can learn. If you have a bad session you can always look back and remind yourself of previous successes.

The other important aspect of evaluation is getting feedback from the young men and I have often found this to be more problematic. As a way of evaluating as I go along, I always allow some time at the end of each session for comments and questions. This opportunity is rarely used. Part of growing up to be a 'man' is needing to be seen to be 'cool', to present a 'take it or leave it' attitude. This makes getting feedback from young men in a group difficult. On an *individual* basis, however, getting feedback can be easier. Workers at the centres where I have run groups often report that young men have approached them *between* sessions to ask questions or make comments. If you are in regular contact with individuals outside the group sessions you may find this is a more appropriate way to get feedback. This may need to be worked at. Generally speaking, though, the more respect we show for what young men are saying the more likely they are to offer feedback.

At the end of a series of sessions I allow some time to review what we have been looking at and encourage comments about their experience of the group as a whole. In addition, I give out evaluation sheets which I ask them to fill in anonymously (see page 39). Again, if you have an ongoing contact with the young men you may find that feedback will filter through over a period of time after the group has ended.

Assessing whether a sex education group has made any difference to behaviour on a long-term basis is difficult to prove. If you are in regular contact with those in the group, and if the sessions form part of a broader strategy for work with young men, then you can keep working with the issues and watching individuals' relationships develop. Evaluating this kind of work, however, is never likely to be a precise science.

Evaluation sheet

This evaluation sheet is a chance for you to say what you feel about the sessions you have taken part in.
Do not add your name to the sheet. In this way you can be as honest as you like and no one will know who wrote it.

Mark an X on the line nearest the end that best describes how you feel about the sessions

Interesting_____Boring

I learned something new_____I learned nothing

Complete the following:

One thing I enjoyed about the sessions was ....

....

....

....

....

What I didn't like about the sessions was ....

....

....

....

....

....

Any other comments ....

....

....

....

Permission is granted to photocopy this page.

Support

Although running a sex eduction group is likely to be a lot of fun, it may also feel like hard work at times. Certainly there will be times when the work forces us to think hard about our own 'manhood' and old fears and emotions re-emerge.

Unfortunately, as men we learn to be independent, forcing ourselves to 'stand on our own two feet', even when others may be willing to co-operate and offer help. Running a group like this may well be a good opportunity to try breaking out of these old habits.

The most obvious support you can get for yourself is by having a co-worker. Together you can plan, prepare, run and evaluate the group. This not only allows you to meet your need for support, for sharing the load, but in addition offers the young men the chance to see two men working together co-operatively and supportively. Of course, it is also possible that workers will have some different values and feelings about sexuality. If these are discussed and made explicit it will be more beneficial to the work. If this is done then differences that come up in the actual groups may be dealt with positively and constructively.

Forming a support group with other men working with young men can provide not only emotional support and reassurance, but also keep you thinking clearly about how the work is going. Similar issues to those found in groups of young men are likely to come up in a group of adult men, such as separation, homophobia, competition and the strangeness of being in an all male group. Because of this it is important that the group have a structure which can deal with these issues. We need to provide for ourselves the same things we are trying to provide for young men. (See *Work with Boys* by Trefor Lloyd for a useful model for support groups.)

By talking about your work and by letting others know what you're doing you will also pick up support. If people know what you are involved in they are less likely to be suspicious and you will probably find that most will be right behind you. In addition, by being proud of your work and saying so you will also be indirectly supporting others who might have been thinking about doing something but had been afraid or felt isolated.

Using resources

Resources are tools, a means to an end, and are useful if they help us achieve our aims. The basic aims of sex education

groups for young men are to impart information and to
encourage free and open discussion about their ideas, feelings,
values and behaviour. Videos, quizzes or games can be useful if
they help bring this about. Resources differ in what they can
help us achieve. Some give information, some make us think,
others challenge, move us or make us laugh. Because of the way
we are brought up as men, one of the most important uses of a
resource is to help break the ice of our 'cool' attitudes and give
us permission to start really communicating with one another.

Bearing in mind the motto that 'resources are a means to an
end', the following are a few suggestions to help you get the
most out of your resources:

- Don't rely on resources as the key to success. Playing a
  video and then sitting back and waiting for a sparkling
  discussion to break out probably won't work. Whatever
  resource you are using, *you* are still the most important
  factor in encouraging communication or in imparting
  information.
- On the other hand, don't be frightened to use resources.
  Young men *will* fill in questionnaires and quizzes if you ask
  them. Some will even attempt role plays. Try things out.
  See what works best for a particular group. I have never yet
  found, for example, a group who refused to play the
  Grapevine Game. You do, however, need to explain *why*
  you are going to do a particular exercise or watch a video.
  Resources used out of context or without explanation can
  confuse or annoy the group.
- Always preview and try out new resources yourself before
  taking them to a group. I speak from bitter experience.
  Some resources in the sex education field are dreadful.
  Some resources may also need to be adapted because they
  are too long or because they don't fully cover the subject
  you want to look at.
- Many resources seem to have been made with an audience
  of polite, white middle-class adults in mind. I have tried to
  recommend resources that represent a range of races, class
  and cultural groups. Unfortunately, these are relatively few
  and far between, although the newer the resources the
  better they tend to be. This is another very good reason for
  carefully previewing and selecting resources you feel will
  suit the group you are going to work with.
- If you are worried about not being able to keep
  conversation flowing then prepare more than enough for
  each session. If you have prepared several resources then

you might avoid a panic when the group whizzes through the quiz in 5 minutes, tells you that the game you have brought in is 'boring', and that they already know everything there is to know above contraceptives. It is not always easy, nor necessarily desirable, to spend the whole of a session 'just talking'. 'Doing something', through the use of resources, is an important safety net for young men who not used to talking.

- Mix your resources. A diet of quizzes every session will quickly lead to boredom.
- Make up your own resources. You will probably have to adapt many resources anyway, and in doing so you may find you produce something more appropriate for the young men you are working with. Try things out. Experiment.

Described below are a variety of resources I have used in Part II of this book. I have tried to keep both the resources I have made up and those I recommend as simple as possible. Most of the time I work with groups where there are different levels of literacy, and so I steer away from more formal methods. (This said, I have always found young men to be very willing to help out a friend who is not comfortable reading or writing.) Obviously each method has its advantages and disadvantages. I suggest you take what you need and adapt them to suit you and the group you are working with. The golden rule is that if it gets young men talking and listening to each other, then use it.

Quizzes

Quizzes are useful not only in terms of imparting information, but also as a way of starting fuller discussions. Inevitably there are associations with 'tests', which can lead to individuals feeling inhibited. Plenty of reassurance is needed that this isn't a competition.

Videos and films

A film can: tell a story, inform, provoke, be fun, be moving. Films or videos, particularly dramas with a story, can get over issues in ways which other resources cannot. Furthermore, watching TV is an activity everyone will be familiar with. Therein also lies its limitations. Watching TV is essentially a self-contained activity, even if done in a group. I have often found that trying to get a coversation going after watching a video is like trying to raise the dead. People switch off while watching and find it hard to switch back to communicating with others once it's over. The most successful way to use videos seems to be either to show them between sessions and discuss later, or show them one week and raise the issues the next. And you do need to follow them with some activity which will raise the issues and clarify information, rather than hope that this will happen spontaneously.

Games

Games are another format that young people are used to and which are often taken up with enthusiasm. People get involved, conversation and argument flows, information is learned and fun is had by all. Obviously you will need to select your game with a particular audience in mind (although something like the 'Grapevine Game' seems to work in almost all circumstances). As with quizzes and discussion cards, a certain level of literacy is required, although as I have said before, I have always found groups of young men to be very understanding and helpful to those whose reading skills are limited.

Slides

These provide visual illustrations and are appealing because young men seem to enjoy sitting in darkened rooms looking at pictures. As with films and videos, slides tend to make conversation more difficult (particularly if you have to darken the room). They work better with lectures rather than group discussions.

Role play

This can be great fun and enormously creative. Potentially it allows individuals to get in touch with their feelings and behaviour in a way other resources do not. The key to its success lies in how trusting and comfortable participants, including the group leader, feel with this kind of thing. Many adult groups I have worked with will only fully participate in role play under duress and it's not something I've used widely with young men. I imagine that the better you know the group and the longer you work with them the more likely this becomes possible.

Discussion or 'trigger' cards

The variations on this theme are endless and I have used them many times in Part II. Discussion cards are statements which invite responses from participants usually aimed at promoting discussion around values, attitudes and feelings. This method requires the leader to make connections, ask supplementary questions, and to encourage sensitively more than just one-word, 'yes' or 'no' answers.

Newspaper and magazine clippings

A good collection of these can be very useful for promoting debate and illustrating the ways in which the media influence our opinions, attitudes and values.

Brainstorming

Brainstorming serves a number of functions: it gets lots of ideas thrown up for discussion quickly, it's a great way to break the ice when a group is just starting and it gets people involved without being under the 'spotlight'. If you use it, try to keep the brainstorm brief, then leave plenty of time to discuss what has been thrown up.

Working informally

You don't have to run a sex education group to raise the issues of sex and sexuality with young men. A group provides a structure and creates a particular kind of environment in which to talk about these issues. If you don't want to run a group you can do this in other ways. Young men's questions, anxieties, attitudes and beliefs about sex come up in the everyday run of things. Discussions happen, questions are asked and answered virtually anywhere, in the minibus, round the camp fire, over the pool table, under the bonnet of a car. Opportunities present themselves all the time.

Because such times are not necessarily pre-planned doesn't mean you can't be prepared. Doing some of the exercises in the appendix or some of the reading on pages 122–6 might be helpful. You might also get together with a colleague and discuss how the young men you work with deal with sex and sexuality and thereby develop strategies through which you can consciously work with these issues. Getting support from colleagues is important as much in 'informal' work as it is in running a group. Isolation is one of the most important ways in which we sabotage our work with young men and end up reacting to their behaviour rather than responding creatively.

Even if you are running a group there is still a place for more informal work outside of sessions. Because of your involvement in a sex education group you may well find yourself approached far more frequently by individuals for advice, or just a chat, on sexual matters. Making yourself available in this way is a good way to complement what happens in the group.

Working with individuals

Although the groups I have been describing are discussion based and not intended to be in any way 'therapeutic' they may, of course, bring up all sorts of feelings and anxieties for individuals which it may not be at all appropriate to deal with in the group. Most of us have experienced some sort of emotional hurt around sex and relationships and for some of us these may be deep rooted and need to be looked at in greater depth. This could range from sexual abuse to someone concerned that they may have an STD. For young men admitting to have a 'problem' like this may be very difficult indeed. It means that you may have to go out of your way to identify yourself as someone 'safe' to go to. Working on this level is not possible in a sex education discussion group since it may require a very high degree of individual attention and trust.

You may be able to offer someone counselling yourself. If you cannot do this then you are in a good position to help this young person find appropriate help. In practice this means not only making yourself available and approachable, but also being aware of what other services are available in your area (see pages 128–32).

Sexual abuse

It's quite possible, either in a group or after, that there may be discussion of sexual abuse. It is important to talk about this in general terms and allow an exploration of young men's attitudes and feelings about it. However, it is also possible that there may be someone in the group who has been abused or is an abuser. For some individuals, such a discussion could be very distressing, and you need to be sensitive to this possibility when the subject comes up.

Such a discussion may lead to you being approached by an individual with a more or less direct request for help. It's a good idea to try and prepare yourself for this eventuality. Let it be known that you have further information, perhaps by putting up some posters with appropriate telephone helpline numbers. Discuss with colleagues in advance 'what you would do if . . .' Because the idea of sexual abuse is shocking, there is a tendency to disbelieve a young person who asks for help and to find reasons why they must be making it up. Listen carefully to them and take what they say at face value, then make sure that the individual is put in touch with someone who is experienced in dealing with sexual abuse. Your reaction is important since you may be the first person they have dared to speak to. Don't panic yourself though by expecting to deal with this on your own. Get appropriate help and you will have done the young person an enormous service. (See pages 128–32 for sources of further information.)

Part II
Doing the work

5 Sessions and resources

In this part of the book you will find sections covering seven broad areas: Introduction, Bodies, Contraception, HIV/AIDS and STDs, Sexuality, Sexism, men and women and Being a man.

These divisions are to some extent arbitrary. They are intended to be used as guidelines for organising the material and the range of issues likely to come up in a series of sessions. They are not meant to be rigid categories by which you are meant to organise a group. In each section, there are likely to be a number of issues which in themselves could form the basis of a separate session. You are in the best position to decide what should be covered. Life does not always follow the neat ordering of 'How to' books like this one. Below I have set out how the sections are organised.

A session

Each session starts with a description of one of a series of sessions I ran with a group of young men on a Youth Training Scheme in North London. The men in the group were aged 17–18 and were a mixture of black (Afro-Caribbean), white, and Greek Cypriot young men. These descriptions hopefully show some of the issues that come up, the problems and the pleasures of this kind of work.

Information

Here I explain what you need to know to get by, giving a summary of the kind of facts you should have a working knowledge of. These are not here to be learned parrot-fashion, but it is a good idea to do a bit of homework to prepare for the sessions.

Reading

This contains some suggestions for background reading for basic information and issues. There is also a list of 'Further reading' for those of you who are really keen.

Resources

This section gives you some ideas for getting started. These suggestions cover a range of activities – quizzes, videos, games, etc. Some of these require a level of literacy, but I suggest mixing these with others that don't. The material is laid out so that you can photocopy the quizzes, diagrams, etc. for your own use. To find out details about books mentioned, and where to get hold of any films, videos or other materials referred to, see pages 122–32.

Many of the resource ideas I have listed will not be new to you. I have 'borrowed' ideas and adapted things to suit my own way of working and the different needs of the young men I have worked with. I have kept the resource ideas simple in the hope that others will adapt and add to suit the different experiences and needs of different groups of young men.

Language

In the exercises I have tried to use language that is commonly understood and accepted by the young men I work with. You may feel you need to change or adapt the language.

Introduction

A session

The room I'm shown into is dark, dingy and filled with cigarette smoke. About 12 young men, white and black, are seated with their backs to the wall, waiting. As I walk in I shake hands with Dave, the Employment Training supervisor who has asked me to come in and who has agreed, hesitantly, to be part of the group in the forthcoming weeks.

I'm a little nervous as always at the start of a new series of sessions, but it helps to remind myself that the rest of them will be a lot more nervous than me. And so it proves to be for as I look around I see 12 unnaturally quiet young men sitting as close to the walls as they can get. All except one, that is, who is moving around and who breaks the silence that has fallen since my arrival with an overloud 'Hello, I'm Tony' and an exaggeratedly friendly handshake. Giggles and jokes follow as this young man becomes the focus for nervous anticipation. I joke back that it's an honour to meet him and the tension eases a bit.

Starting a new group is often like this, nobody knows what to expect. Sex education – is it about mating rabbits, diagrams, or how to do 'it'? And underlying all of this is the unfamiliarity, for men, of sitting down in a group and talking with each other.

I start by asking them if any of them had any sex education before. Few have, it seems, and it's been mostly 'biological'. I ask who else they learned from: older brothers, friends, parents? Silence. There are two young men who have said something so far. I look at them and they respond hesitantly. The others are still staring at their shoelaces with a new found fascination. They laugh when Tony and another boy say something. 'They're just little kids,' says Tony to me in a man-to-man sort of way.

I stick a large sheet of paper on the wall and write 'sex' on it. The reason I do this is because young people grow up being taught that sex is bad, naughty, dirty, and that it's everywhere. Young men, when they do talk about sex, use it as a weapon, to shock (adults), to compete (with male friends), to impress and oppress (young women). By getting them to say all the words they know to do with sex, and by writing them up on the paper, I'm hoping to undercut some of these behaviours, so they can both talk and listen to each other and feel more comfortable with me.

The words of the young men come slowly at first, then faster with giggles, with a leer, with embarrassment, with daring. After 10 minutes or so of this, the atmosphere has lightened considerably. I ask them whether any of the words they have suggested might offend anyone – women, gay men, lesbians, parents, teachers? Inveitably there are those who talk and those who listen. I make a mental note of who they are. The 'talkers' are getting into it now. In fact, one of them can hardly be stopped. Tony wants to tell us all about his sexual exprinces. At first he's listened to but the others soon become fed up with his boasting and try to shut him up. However, at least he's talking, although I need to be careful not to let him and a couple of others dominate. Having been shut up by the others he starts to ask me about my sexual life. 'You're the expert. How do you please a woman?' He's semi-serious. He denies suggestions from the others about whether he 'has a problem'. I tell him that I'm not an 'expert' and that I'm not here to instruct anybody how to 'do it'. Much laughter and catcalls follow.

I need to be careful at times like this. Partly this is a set-up, i.e. 'Let's get this sex-guy to talk about "doing it" and have a few laughs.' Partly this young man is genuine: he has some anxiety about his sexual 'performance', as many young and adult men do.

I start talking about the pressure we are often under to have sex, that maybe sex doesn't need to be a performance, and how there's no 'right' way to 'do it'. They look puzzled. This is obviously as difficult for them to take in as it is for me to try and explain. For most men sex is a performance: you have got to learn to do as well in this as you have at work, or at playing football, or drinking or fighting. In the following weeks we keep coming back to this issue, with the young men finding new ways to ask the same question, and voice the same fear.

Because this is the first session I want the conversation to be as wide-ranging as possible in order that the group get a sense of the possible areas we could talk about in the following weeks. I get out the Grapevine Game and because there are so many of them I divide them into pairs. This works really well. The game is an excellent tool for bringing up a range of subjects. Some of the questions provoke heated discussions, others are passed over fairly quickly. Where there is fear and embarrassment I have to do a lot of prompting and coaxing, asking questions. Sometimes there is just not enough trust and it feels like really hard work.

In the group some are very vocal and at ease in giving their opinion on issues, others are not. I make sure that those who up until now have been quiet, speak and get listened to. I explain as we start the game this this is a chance for everyone to have a say and an opportunity to hear others talk. Inevitably, though, for some it is very difficult and my prompting and protecting has little effect.

My other agenda in using the game is to get a chance to gauge the level of factual knowledge in the group. This helps to plan future sessions. In this group, for example, their factual knowledge about AIDS was quite good but there was misunderstanding about other STDs.

A question comes up on homosexuality and a range of views from 'I don't mind what they do. It's their business isn't it.' to 'Hang 'em. This AIDS business is all their fault.' I push them a bit, asking 'Why do you feel like that?' 'What if your brother told you he was gay?' 'Some of us here might be gay, don't you think?' After a few attempts by some of them to have the definitive word, they are keen to move on. I say that we will come back to this issue in another session.

Talking about homosexuality brings up young men's

defensive attitudes more readily than anything else. The fear and anxiety in the room is almost tangible. I believe that many young men's fear of gay men is based on a deep-rooted fear of other men and a fragile sense of what 'being a man' is all about. The subject of homosexuality only serves to bring to the surface what is there all the time. In fact, easing this fear is my main aim in working with any group of men.

Another question comes up, this time asking what makes a good parent. It provokes a heated and lengthy discussion. Tony and a couple of others come from Greek-Cypriot families, and they quickly find themselves under fire from the others for their 'strict' and 'old-fashioned' views. They become very defensive. I try reminding them that we are here to listen to each other and talk about things without having to attack each other. I try to shift the focus away from a slanging match by asking them specific questions about their family values and how they feel about them, and what they think is important. Then, in order to take the heat off them I ask the others to think about what their family and culture has taught them. What were they taught about families and marriage and being a parent? What do they feel like when someone attacks their beliefs and traditions? One young white man says he doesn't want anything to do with what his parents believe in, saying 'I'm gonna live how I like.' My questions don't get answered as the argument polarises once again into 'There's no argument. I'm right, you're wrong, let's leave it at that.'

The question of loyalty to family and cultural traditions surfaced several times in this group. It is difficult for all of us to be able to both question and value our heritage and become confident in our own sense of what is right and wrong. Young people in general are not encouraged to develop their own sense of responsibility, particularly around issues concerning sex and relationships. The young Greek-Cypriot and black men in this group also have to contend with a society whose racism further devalues their own experience and heritage. Because we were a group of men the discussion quickly became polarised, one side taking a pro-family position, the other a pro-individual position. Nobody wanted to 'back-down' and lose face. The hardest thing for this group was to look at an issue without it becoming a confrontation where somebody had to lose.

What I try to do in this kind of situation is remind them that it's not a battle and suggest that it might be possible to talk without there having to be winners and losers. This, of course, is the real substance of the work since this pattern emerges whatever the topic.

After a while some of them decide that they have had enough of this and tell the others to 'shut up so we can finish the game'. The game comes to a close and the session finishes. It's lasted just over an hour. They now have an idea of what this 'sex education business' is all about, and I have a sense of the issues I will need to focus on in the coming weeks. The session has been lively, to say the least, and this I am grateful for as it is not always the case. They have sat and talked and to some extent listened to each other for over an hour on subjects they may never have had the opportunity to seriously look at before.

First sessions are often the most exciting if they get going. Later the going can get tough when the initial rush of excitement is over. When established views have been repeatedly challenged and old fears stirred up, the defensive walls can easily be re-established. Because of this process, it's important that those who are in regular daily contact with young people become able to deal with these issues themselves.

I end my visit with a 10-minute chat with Dave, the supervisor, reviewing what happened. He says he will canvass those who were in the group to get some feedback on how they feel it went.

Information

No specialised factual information is particularly required here. The answers to questions in the Grapevine Game recommended below are in the booklet provided with it. Make sure you have played it beforehand to familiarise yourself.

Reading

Basic

Jane Cousins, *Make it Happy*

Further

Ruth Bell (ed.), *Changing Bodies, Changing Lives*
Trefor Lloyd, *Work with Boys*

Resources

1   I always ask two questions of the group which help to put into context what follows:
- What kind of sex education have you had?
- Where did you learn what you know about sex?

2   Brainstorm **sex, love, relationships**

Aims

This exercise is useful in a number of ways. It sets out the range of possible topics to be covered in the following sessions. It is also a way of dealing straight away with any embarrassment and fear young men may have in talking about sex without putting pressure on any particular individual. It also gives the group a chance to see that I am not going to be 'shocked' by what they say.

How to use

Write 'sex' on a large sheet of paper (which can be saved for other exercises later) and get everybody to shout out their suggestions. I say that I will write anything down and that they should use whatever language they feel comfortable with. When this is done I go through what is written down talking about language and asking if any of them find any words offensive. I then ask if, say, women, or parents, or teachers or gay men, for example, would find any of the words offensive. Try and encourage discussion about what our language says about how we feel about sex.

3   The Grapevine Game. See pages 127–8.

Bodies

A session

'Are we going to play that game again?' asks one young man with guarded enthusiasm as I walk in.

'Well no, actually' I reply, somewhat surprised at his question since he had been very quiet during the first session. 'I thought we'd have a look at bodies this week.' This gets a few catcalls and whistles.

'Have you brought in a woman then?' says another young man who last week had been insistent that a sex education group should mean a practical demonstration of 'doing it'.

'No. Today's a chance for you to find out how much you know about your own and women's bodies.'

'Yeah, well I already know all I need to know from practical experience, thanks very much,' says Tony.

I hand out two sheets of papers, one a cut-away diagram of the male genitals and one of the female.

'We've done all this in biology' complains Derek's mate Chris.

'Good. Then you'll be able to tell the rest of us all about it.' I ask them to go through each and identify all the 'bits'.

I'm starting with the 'mechanics', because for many young men, it's likely to be one of the few areas (along with contraception and STDs) in which they have had any experience of sex education. For many young men, especially an older age group like this, it might be seen to be an insult to be learning the 'facts of life' at so late a stage in life. It is here that a 'seen it, done it, been there' attitude is likely to emerge. But unfortunately, many haven't, and for those who have retained something, the connection between the 'facts' and their own experience is tenuous. A basic understanding of these facts is crucial to many of the other topics we will be looking at later.

'I don't look like that, do I?' says one young man.

'I'm afraid you do, and unless you want to cut yourself in half you'll have to take my word for it', I tell him. We go through the diagrams, starting with the man's, and identify the parts and what they do.

With a look of nervous concern on his face Tony says, 'I've heard of this geezer, right, and his is 2 foot long.'

'That's 2 foot longer than yours, then,' quips Chris.

'Shut up, I'm asking a serious question here. I mean . . .' his voice trails off, 'wouldn't he hurt a woman. I mean it's not size that counts, is it?'

It is clear that men worry about their penises, an anxiety that is reflected in the amount of time we spend trying to convince each other that ours is bigger than anyone else's. Yet few of us will admit to having looked at another man's to compare. Being unable to talk about our penises and other parts of our bodies because of this competitiveness means we are unable to get reassurance by comparing notes.

A sharp discussion about penis size and 'pleasing a woman' follows amid much giggling, laughing and teasing of Tony. I say that it's a good question since all men tend to worry about size and whether they are good lovers or not. We move on to the diagram of the woman's genitals. I ask people to name the parts they know. Several are able to identify the labia and the vagina but find the rest a bit of a mystery. One young man, Gary, who has been quiet up to now is able to fill in the rest. He obviously paid attention during school biology. 'You've been doing your homework, haven't you,' says Chris with a look of reluctant admiration on his face. As we go through the diagram several young men visibly flinch as I describe what all the 'parts' are for.

I do this because many young men grow up with a fear of women. Squeamishness and ignorance about women's bodies sit side by side with their attraction to them. Menstruation is often the focus for this. Looking at diagrams, learning the facts, and talking about how they feel is a good start in demystifying what they see as 'women's business'.

'What's the clitoris for, then?' someone asks.

'It's where the woman get her enjoyment from,' says 'quiet' Gary, unprompted.

Admiration increases further. I encourage him to say more but the newfound attention is too much and he dries up. I help him by asking him questions and filling in any missing bits, telling them that 'yes', the clitoris is important as is the rest of the genital area. The others are all listening, open-mouthed and wide-eyed. It's a wonderful moment. The know-it-all 'front' has dropped and they genuinely want to know. Gary's standing in the group has rocketed.

In an effort to keep the momentum going I follow this up by asking them what an orgasm is. Tony and Chris start confidendly answering me with a 'this-is-so-obvious-why-are-you-asking-us' tone in their voice. 'It's when you come, innit.' 'You know – do it', 'Spunk up', 'Whooah you know'. But they get stuck when I ask them to describe it. 'What does it feel like?' They look perplexed and slightly embarrassed. I ask them to have a think about it for next week.

Our lack of language about sex and our lack of commun-ication show when asked this kind of question. For all the bluff and bluster about sex, when it comes down to saying how we really feel we get stuck. Talking about great pleasure is just as difficult for young men as expressing their sadness or pain.

I move on by saying that I'm sure we all know how a baby is born, but would someone like to explain it just for the record. 'You tell us, Gary' says Chris, 'since you seem to know everything else'. Gary goes through the details after some prompting from me, making only a couple of 'mistakes'. I congratulate him. I then ask if anybody has any questions, but there is no response.

This is probably because the process of pregnancy and birth hold little interest for young men, except perhaps for younger boys and some who may be fathers. Squeamishness about women's bodies obviously plays a part in this, but it is also connected with an attitude that anything to do with children is women's business and nothing to do with us.

It's been a fact-packed section, and I resist the temptation to try and fit in something on puberty. Sometimes I have to let go of my desire to go through it all. Despite the slow start the session has gone pretty well. I hang around in case anybody wants to ask anything.

Information

Basic anatomy of the genital and reproductive system, both male and female; conception, pregnancy and birth; the menstrual cycle; pubertal changes; sexual response, both male and female.

Reading

Basic

Jane Cousins, *Make It Happy*
Ruth Bell (ed.), *Changing Bodies, Changing Lives*
B. Zilbergeld, *Men and Sex*

Further

A. Phillips & J. Rakusen (eds.), *Our Bodies Our Selves*
The Hite Report on Male Sexuality
The Hite Report on Female Sexuality

Resources

1   Family Planning Association, 'Male' and 'Female' cards

2   'Sexuality and the Mentally Handicapped' – slides by Winifred Kempton

3   'The First Days Of Life' – film

4   'Am I Normal?' – film

5   Male and female diagrams

Aims

To give clear, accurate information on male and female genitals, on reproduction and sexual response

How to use

Photocopy diagrams and get individuals to put a name
(their own words and not necessarily medical terms) to the
numbered parts.

The diagrams are set out on page 60.

6   Body quiz

Aims

To correct myths and give clear accurate information about
our bodies.

How to use

Get individuals or pairs to fill in and then go through in
group.

The quiz and answers are set out on pages 62–3.

7   'When you were 9 . . .' questionnaire

Aims

To highlight and encourage thought and discussion around
the changes, emotional as well as physical, brought on by
puberty.

How to use

Get individuals to fill in the questionnaire answering the
questions for when they were aged 9 and now. Go through
and compare the answers in the group. What are the
significant differences? Are you the same kind of person
then and now? What difference has puberty made?

The questionnaire is set out on page 65.

Male pelvic organs

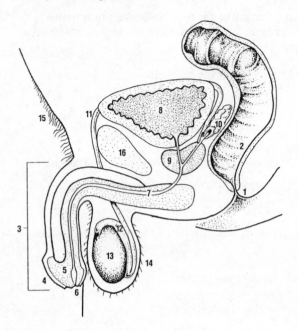

Female pelvic organs

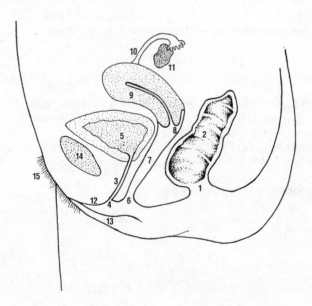

Male and female diagrams – answers

Female pelvic organs				*Male pelvic organs*			
1	Anus	9	Uterus	1	Anus	9	Prostate gland
2	Rectum	10	Fallopian tube	2	Rectum	10	Seminal vesicle
3	Urethra	11	Ovary	3	Penis	11	Vas deferens
4	Urethral opening	12	Clitoris	4	Foreskin	12	Epididymus
5	Bladder	13	Vaginal lips	5	Glans	13	Testicle
6	Vaginal opening	14	Pubic bone	6	Urethral opening	14	Scrotum
7	Vagina	15	Pubic hair	7	Urethra	15	Pubic hair
8	Cervix			8	Bladder	16	Pubic bone

Body quiz

1 For every 100 female babies there are
   a) 95
   b) 100
   c) 105
   male babies born

2 An erection is
   a) when the penis fills with blood
   b) when a bone inside the penis stiffens
   c) when the penis is full of semen
   d) when we vote in a new government

3 The average length of an erect (hard) penis is:
   a) 4½"
   b) 5"
   c) 6"
   d) 9"

4 The average length of a non-erect (soft) penis is:
   a) 2"
   b) 3½"
   c) 5"
   d) 6"

5 The average length of the vagina is:
   a) 3½"
   b) 4½"
   c) 5"
   d) 6"

6 The only way to stop balding is to:
   a) wear a hat
   b) stop worrying
   c) be castrated

7 The average male produces how much semen (spunk)
   when he ejaculates (comes)?
   a) a teaspoonful
   b) a dessertspoonful
   c) a cup full

Permission is granted to photocopy pages 62–3.

8 How many sperm does a man release each time he
   ejaculates?
   a) 20,000
   b) 100,000
   c) 1 million
   d) 200–300 million

9 The testicles are on the outside of the body because:
   a) sperm need to be kept cooler than the normal body
       temperature
   b) there isn't room for them inside

10 The bleeding during a woman's period lasts from
    a) 2–3 hours
    b) 2–8 days
    c) 5 minutes a day

11 From what age does a girl have eggs in her ovaries?
    a) 12
    b) 13
    c) 16
    d) birth

12 The clitoris is situated:
    a) at the top of the vulva
    b) between the anus and the vagina
    c) inside the vagina

13 Which of the following are erogenous zones (areas of the
    body which make us feel sexually aroused when touched):
    a) lips
    b) nipples
    c) ear lobes
    d) big toe

14 A woman cannot get pregnant if:
    a) she has sex during her period
    b) she has sex standing up
    c) she is having sexual intercourse for the first time
    d) she is a lesbian

15 A 'wet dream' is:
    a) ejaculating (coming) during your sleep
    b) peeing in the bed in your sleep
    c) dreaming about swimming

Body quiz – answers

1   (a)

2   (a) In fact *women* could also be said to have 'erections' since the same process occurs when blood rushes into the area around the clitoris and the labia when they are sexually aroused.

3   (b)(c) The average is between 5–6". It's worth emphasising that this is only an average, i.e. some will be smaller and some larger.

4   (b) Again this is only an average.

5   (b)

6   (c) I'm afraid so!

7   (b) Again this is only an average.

8   (d)

9   (a)

10   (b)

11   (d)

12   (a) It's worth noting that although the clitoris is very important in terms of women's sexual arousal, the *whole* area around the top of the vulva is highly sensitive.

13   All or none of them. Whatever turns you on!

14   None of these. It is possible to get pregnant during a period. She certainly can get pregnant if she has sex standing up or if it's the first time. Only successful use of contraception would prevent conception. And finally, a lesbian woman could get pregnant through AID (Artificial Insemination by Donor) – and many do.

15   (a)

'When you were 9' – a questionnaire

	Age 9	Now

1   What year was it?

2   What height were you?

3   Who won (will win) the FA Cup?

4   What was the name of your best mate?

5   Did you have spots or acne?

6   Did you have hair around your genitals?

7   Who was the Prime Minister?

8   Did you know the 'Facts of Life'?

9   Did you have sexual feelings?

10   Did you cry?

11   Did you wear short trousers?

12   Were your friends boys, girls or both?

Contraception

A session

'Any questions from last time?' I ask hopefully. Nothing.
'Anything you'd particularly like to talk about today?' Nothing.
They seem flat and uninterested, even Tony who usually has
something to say on every subject. 'OK. Suppose you've
decided you are going to have sex and you know you're not
ready to be a parent yet. What do you do?'

'Johnnies,' says Chris without enthusiasm. 'Yeah. Anything
else?'

'Cap.' 'Pill.' 'Pull it out quick.'

'That's useless,' says Tony, 'there's no pleasure in that'.

'And it doesn't work,' I add. 'Even if you come just outside
the vagina, there's still a chance that the sperm will get inside.'
There are a couple of worried faces now. 'Anybody heard
anything else like that?'

Contraception is a minefield of dangerous myths. You can't
get pregnant doing it standing up, or the first time, or if she
doesn't come, or during a period, etc. Much of this is due to a
lack of clear, straightforward information, but there is also an
element of wishful thinking on the part of men.

'Sheaths, cap, pill – anybody know any other methods?' I ask.
Silence. I pull out the bag of contraceptives and open it up.
Eyes widen and they all pull in to have a closer look. 'What is
the only method aimed at men?'

'Durex,' comes the cry.

'Has anybody not seen one?' The hands stay down.

'So everyone knows how to use them.' Smiles and sniggers.
'Would anyone like to put one on . . .' I pause for effect and
everyone draws back a little, 'this pen?'

'No problem. I've had plenty of practice,' says Tony
inevitably. He proceeds to flamboyantly open the packet and
then fumbles it clumsily onto the fat felt-tip pen. I appreciate
him for being brave enough to demonstrate and ask for
comments from the others.

'She'd have gone to sleep waiting for you,' says one boy.

I go through what Tony did saying what he did well and
correcting his 'mistakes'. The condom gets passed round, but
thankfully they resist the temptation to blow it up.

'They're horrible, anyway. I wouldn't use them. It's up to the
girl really,' says Chris.

'Well what would the girl use?' I ask him.

'I dunno, pill I suppose. It's nothing to do with me, is it.'

This discussion reflects the fact that male attitudes to contraception in the eighties are a legacy of the changes of the 'permissive' sixties. The pill was the most efficient form of contraception ever and ushered in an era of sexual 'freedom', freedom that is for men rather than for women. For men the pill meant no fuss, no interruptions, and no responsibility. Twenty-five years on long term pill-users are still counting the cost of this 'freedom' in the shape of increased susceptibility to cancer and a host of other side-effects. Historically, efforts to improve contraception have focused on better technology to improve the efficiency of methods aimed at women. Far less emphasis has been placed on improving the way we deal with the methods we already have. Ignorance plays its part, but men's reluctance to get involved also stems from deep-seated attitudes about women and sex.

We talk about responsibility. To my surprise about half the group claim that they think it's just as much to do with the man as the woman. I ask how many of them carry condoms if they think they might be going to have sex. They look at each other before three or four of them tentatively raise their hands. I ask if any of them think contraception is wrong morally. Nobody says anything and I explain that some religions say that you shouldn't use anything. If anybody does have feelings about this they're not going to expose themselves.

'Yeah, but you've got to use a condom now because of AIDS,' says one young man, Errol, who has been looking rather worried since the beginning.

'But they get in the way! Just when you're getting down to some real action, you're not gonna stop and say "Excuse me, I must put my condom on now, if you don't mind," ' says Chris, acting out a polite mime of putting a condom on. He gets laughter of recognition and embarrassment for his performance, and a discussion about 'how' and 'when' follows.

It seems that for most young men, sex is something you do, not something you talk about. If you don't know something then you act as if you do. In order to be able to take responsibility for contraception, young men have to learn to become more comfortable talking about sex (and they must be encouraged to find out the facts when there is a gap in their knowledge). Talking about sex means talking about how you feel, and again, this is not something young men are encouraged to do. To complicate things further sex is supposed to be 'spontaneous', it just happens and once the process is started it is somehow unstoppable. 'Taking responsibility' is usually seen as something negative, especially by young men.

This needs to be reframed. Without talking, safer sex practices become very difficult. Talking about sex could help save our lives. But put more positively, talking can be presented as a way of both partners getting more of what they want. No unwanted parenthood, no hurt or angry partner, no upset family and a better and more relaxed, safer, more fulfilled sex life. What more could you want?

'Well, what about methods women can use. What do you know about them?' I ask. We talk about the pill and two or three young men comment that it's dangerous and that girls shouldn't use it. I ask how many would use a male pill if it was available. No volunteers. I pull out the cap and demonstrate its use and pass it round to much giggling. They put it on their heads, over their noses, but all refuse to touch the spermicide that goes with it. The coil genuinely shocks and puzzles them. I use last session's diagrams to show how it gets used. We talk through all the methods, looking at the advantages and disadvantages.

'But none of them are a 100 per cent sure, are they?' says the worried looking Errol. Someone says that there is always abortion if you get caught out. This unleashes a short but furious debate. Both Tony and Chris are adamant. 'It's murder.' Some of the others say it's nothing to do with them, it's the girl's responsibility. I try to make sure everyone gets a say and that all opinions get listened to, but it's hard.

Young men are usually ignorant of what an abortion involves and what it may mean to women. This is true both of those with strongly held moral or religious beliefs and those for whom it is a convenience. Talking about abortion can be a way to bring home some of the wider issues about male responsibility.

It's time to finish and as the group leave Errol, who has been looking anxious throughout, hangs back. We spend some time talking. He's been having sex and not using contraceptives. I arrange for him to go to the local Brook Advisory Centre.

Information

Basic anatomy – various methods of contraception, pros and cons, and where to get them – local agencies for referral.

Reading

Basic

Jane Cousins, *Make It Happy*
Ruth Bell (ed.), *Changing Bodies, Changing Lives*

Further

Phillips & Rakusen, *Our Bodies Ourselves*
B. Zilbergeld, *Men And Sex*

Resources

1   'Danny's Big Night' – video

2   Contraceptive kit

Aims

To clarify information and dispel myths. To encourage young men to see that contraceptives are not just 'women's business', but are directly relevant to them.

How to use

Go through each method in turn, answering questions and allowing individuals to touch the various contraceptives. There will be plenty of giggling and embarrassment. This is a good opportunity to let all this out.

3   Condoms

Aims

To ensure that young men are familiar with the only form of contraceptive aimed directly at them; to ease fears and embarrassment.

How to use

Get a volunteer to put a condom on . . . a fat pen or a carrot (giggle, giggle, snigger, snigger). Someone usually thinks they know how. Make sure any 'errors' are corrected.

4   'Surprise package'

Aims

To encourage discussion of feelings and attitudes towards condoms.

How to use

Put condoms in sealed envelopes and give one to each individual, then ask for their first reaction upon opening the envelope.

5   Male and female diagrams (see page 60)
     These may be needed to explain how contraceptive methods work.

6   Contraception – What do you think? How do you feel? What would you do?

Aims

To encourage thought and discussion about feelings and opinions about condom use in actual relationships.

How to use

Print questions on to cards and get each group member to pick up one in turn. Encourage discussion on each point.

Questions

•   When is the right time to talk about contraception with a partner?

•   A male pill has been invented. Scientists and doctors say it's safe. Would you take it?

•   You are going out with someone you really fancy on a 'first date'. Would you take condoms with you 'just in case'?

- A friend tells you he's been having sexual intercourse but not using contraception. He says he's 'careful'. Would you say anything to him?

- What do you think about young women under 16 going on the pill. What about someone you were going out with? What about your sister?

- The condom you were using last night broke. Your girlfriend is worried she might be pregnant. What would you do?

- You are going out with someone you really like but she won't use contraceptives because of her religion. How would you feel? What would you do?

- You want to have sex but you don't want to use a condom. On the other hand you don't want to get someone pregnant, nor catch the HIV virus. What could you do?

- A friend tells you it's OK not to use contraceptives if you have sex standing up. What do you think?

- Are you ready to be a father?

- You've been going out with your girlfriend for a couple of months but you haven't had sexual intercourse yet. You discover a packet of condoms in her handbag. How would you react?

HIV/AIDS and STDs (Sexually transmitted diseases)

A session

'Is it the real thing this week,' Chris asks with a leer. 'You know, positions and all that?'

'I can tell you everything you need to know, don't worry about it,' says Tony. I tell him he'll have to find out that sort of thing in his own time. I suggest that we talk about AIDS instead, just to find out what they know.

A collective groan goes up. 'Not again. Bloody AIDS. On the telly, in the papers.'

'It's boring,' says Chris, 'we've done all that.'

I carry on, asking them what is the first thing that comes to mind when they hear the word AIDS. 'Being dead.' 'Queers.' 'Junkies.' 'Nothing – I don't think about it.' 'Boring, boring, boring.'

In popular imagination AIDS = death, and these young men's seeming indifference is a way to cope with this possibility. Fear is manifested in the boredom of 'it can't touch me' and in the rebellion of 'I'm gonna go out enjoying myself'. It's not likely in a group like this that we will get to deal with out deeper fears about death, but it is possible to deal with some of these manifestations. I try to look at the panic, prejudice, fear of sex and the confusion and put them into some kind of perspective.

I persevere, asking them how it's caught, what the difference is between the virus and AIDS. Do they know the symptoms? They decide to humour me and I find that on the whole they are quite well informed.

It seems that much of the factual information about AIDS has got across and a lot of the original myths have been exploded. Yet doctors and scientists are presenting us with new information all the time and consequently young people, like everybody else, need to be kept up to date. What is just as important, and harder to do, is to explore young men's feelings and attitudes to sex. It is only by doing this that they will be able to learn how to protect themselves.

'Where did it come from, though. I mean, somebody must have started it.' says Tony.

'Queers', 'Monkeys', 'African innit' volunteer the group.

'That's just rubbish,' says Lawrence, a young black man.

I tell them that nobody knows where it came from and anyway, nobody asks where the common cold comes from or whose fault it is. I suggest that people want to know because they want to blame someone, like black Africans or gay men, but that it is just a disease.

Although the initial hysteria of 'Gay Plague' headlines has died down, HIV/AIDS is still fuel for prejudice against gay men. In a similar way, reports that the virus has been active in certain parts of Africa for a number of years led to a belief that AIDS 'started' there, is worse there and is somehow the 'fault' of black

Africans. It is important to be able to provide information which contradicts the hysteria and distortions of the media and which fuels this kind of racism.

'But there's no cure, is there', Tony is building up a head of steam, 'and I saw on telly a programme about how some bloke was going around deliberately giving it to other people! They should be shot.'

A discussion follows about what they would do if they found they had the virus. 'I'd top myself.' 'No way! I'd screw as many girls as I could.' (Nervous laughter follows, then quiet.)

Lawrence says, 'You might as well give up.' More quiet.

I explain that having the virus doesn't mean you're going to die tomorrow or even that you will die. They seem unimpressed by this. I turn the conversation round by suggesting that there's lots of ways you can protect yourself.

'Yeah, give up sex,' says Lawrence. I suggest that it needn't be so drastic and ask if anyone has any other suggestions.

'Stick to one partner.' 'Use a condom.'

In the short term, what young men need are practical and accessible ways of protecting themselves and partners from the virus. Safer sex practices – which come up later – are, realistically, a long-term goal. As a starting point we are talking about encouraging the use of condoms. Long since dismissed by men as being an embarrassment, or 'like wearing a raincoat in a shower', they have come back into fashion – in theory at least. Young men still have difficulty with the practice, both in terms of how and when.

The discussion continues. I remind the group how the virus is transmitted and introduce the idea of 'safer sex'. This is met with some scepticism. We go through the original brainstorm we did on 'Sex' and highlight all the 'safer' options.

'But what's the point if you're not gonna do the business?' says Chris.

'It's kids' stuff,' says Tony. 'I'll take my chances.'

The others are silent and look slightly puzzled. Dave, the supervisor, says that he now finds all the other bits of lovemaking more enjoyable than intercourse itself. They look unconvinced but want to know more. Dave, bravely, is a little more specific but refuses requests to deliver the 'juicy details'.

Persuading young men that sexual activity can be enjoyable without full intercourse as its goal is not easy. Most of us have been brought up to believe that 'real' sex = intercourse and anything else is relegated to 'foreplay', a preliminary to the main event. The idea of 'giving up' intercourse, particularly to heterosexual men, is like giving up sex itself. Sex is so tied up with performance and competition – and this can apply to gay men too – with proving ourselves, that to give it up means giving up a particular way of being a man. It is significant that it is gay men who have succeeded in making changes in their sexual lives. They have been more willing to question sterotypes that surround male sexuality. As with other issues, safer sex means learning to talk about sex. This, too, poses a fundamental threat to the current definitions of our manhood. Safer sex means negotiating the use of condoms, asking questions, saying what you want, how you feel, etc.

'It's all right for you lot,' Tony says, looking at me and Dave, 'you've had your fun. What about us?' Neither of us have an answer.

It is easy to get discouraged when dealing with AIDS and, particularly, in trying to promote safer sex. However, it is important to remember that it may in fact be easier for younger men to adopt safer sex practices than those who are a little bit older. Although intercourse remains the ultimate goal for most young men, it remains just that for some time – an ultimate goal. Adolescence is about experimenting, and full sexual intercourse is by no means the norm in all adolescent relationships. Many young people are already practising 'safer sex', even if it is seen as a step towards 'the real thing'. Learning to value what used to be called 'petting' as part of sexual activity might be a realistic step for many young people.

I bring out the STDs cards in an effort to lighten things up. These get taken fairly lightly, an antidote to the gloom and doom of AIDS. There is much jibing, giggling and mock disgust. Other STDs seem trivial in comparison.

'What would you do if you thought you had caught something?' I ask.

'Go to your doctor,' someone suggests.

'Oh yeah, and what's your mum gonna think. Everyone on the estate's gonna know,' says Tony. 'I wouldn't tell no one.'

I remind them about STD clinics and ask if anyone has ever been to one. They are all affronted by my suggestion. Dave, the supervisor, says he has been. They are amazed and jokingly recoil away from him. 'What have you got, Dave?' 'Don't come near me!' 'Does your wife know?' Dave very honestly tells them what he had and what happens at the clinic. They all listen intently to his 'confession'. He is very reassuring but they don't seem convinced. They are particularly shocked at the idea of female doctors examining them. Then they're shocked at the idea of male doctors examining them.

Other STDs are still more common than the HIV virus and if

no longer deadly, then they are still unpleasant. Pre-AIDS, a big issue was the shame and embarrassment young men felt about catching STDs and dealing with them once caught. The fear of death may have superceded these concerns, but they do still exist and STDs still feed into the notion of sex as something 'dirty' and punishable.

'Is that where you get the AIDS test then?' Errol asks.

I explain the difference once again between HIV and AIDS and explain some of the issues about testing. A conversation follows about whether it's better to know or not.

Information

Transmission of HIV and other STDs and symptoms; testing pros and cons and how to use clinics; brief history and basic knowledge of HIV/AIDS statistics in Britain and worldwide; safer sex practices; how to use and where to get condoms.

Reading

Basic

P. Aggleton, C. Horsley, T. Wilton, I. Warwick, *AIDS – Working with Young People*
Terence Higgins Trust leaflets

Further

The National AIDS Manual
AIDS UK
R. Shilts, *And The Band Played On*
P. Gordon & L. Mitchell, *Safer Sex: A New Look at Sexual Pleasure*
C. Spence, *AIDS: Time To Reclaim Our Power*
R.C. & R.J. Chiramuuta, *AIDS, Africa And Racism*
P. Aggleton *et al.* (eds.), *Learning About Aids*
Doreen Massey, *Teaching About HIV and AIDS*

Resources

1   'Coming Soon' – video

2   Condoms
    Same exercises as on page 69.

3   Surprise packages
    Same exercise as on page 70.

4   Safer sex brainstorm

Aims

To get the group thinking about all the different things we mean by sex and which of those might be considered 'safer'.

How to use

To ask the group to suggest all the ways people can have sex which, to their knowledge, are safer. You might want to compare this to the brainstorm done in the introductory session. Another way of doing this is to write 'no risk', 'low risk', 'medium risk', and 'high risk' on a sheet of paper and get the group to indicate which sexual activities fall into which category.

What you will need

Large sheets of paper and felt-tip pens.

5   HIV/AIDS quiz

Aims

To convey some basic general information and to correct myths.

How to use

Give each individual (or pair) a copy to fill in and then go through in the group.

The quiz is set out on pages 78–9.

6   Negotiating safer sex

Aims

To encourage thought and discussion on feelings and the behaviour involved in trying to integrate safer sex into our lives.

How to use

Write out the questions onto cards and get each group member to read one out in turn. Encourage discussion. This exercise is set out on pages 82–3.

7   Match but don't catch! STDs and their symptoms

Aims

To give accurate information about STDs.

How to use

Write the name of diseases on one set of cards and the symptoms on another. Spread on the table and get individuals to try and match a disease to its symptoms. This exercise is set out on pages 83–4.

HIV/AIDS quiz: facts and attitudes

Place a tick next to the correct answer. (There may be more than one answer or there may be no right answer.)

1 You can get the HIV virus from:

☐ toilet seats
☐ sharing needles
☐ having sex with an infected person
☐ kissing
☐ swimming in a public swimming pool
☐ going to the dentist
☐ using someone else's toothbrush
☐ sharing a glass or canned drink
☐ having a blood transfusion

☐ having many sexual partners
☐ masturbation (solo or mutual)
☐ mosquitos
☐ sharing razors
☐ having a tattoo done
☐ having your ears pierced
☐ using drugs
☐ getting a love bite
☐ giving blood
☐ giving first aid
☐ mouth-to-mouth resuscitation

2 The following groups have a higher risk of catching the virus:

☐ gay men
☐ heterosexuals
☐ haemophiliacs
☐ lesbians
☐ young people

☐ prostitutes
☐ drug users
☐ Africans
☐ bisexuals
☐ none of these

3 The HIV virus and AIDS originally came from:

☐ Haiti
☐ San Francisco
☐ The CIA
☐ The KGB

☐ Africa
☐ green monkeys
☐ outer Space
☐ none of these

4 You can get a test:

☐ from your own doctor
☐ from the chemist

☐ at a family planning clinic
☐ from an STD (VD) clinic

5   If someone has the HIV virus:

☐ they are dangerous
☐ they should not give
   blood
☐ they will die

☐ they should not have
   babies
☐ they should not have sex
☐ the are infectious

6   The following symptoms show that a person has AIDS:

☐ persistant fatigue
☐ weight loss
☐ purple blotches on the
   skin
☐ diarrhoea
☐ all of these

☐ fever, chills and night
   sweats
☐ swollen glands
☐ white spots in the mouth
☐ dry cough
☐ none of these

7   If someone has AIDS:

☐ the should not have sex
☐ they should be isolated
☐ none of these

☐ they are going to die
☐ they should stop work
☐ all of these

8   Who should you tell if you have the HIV virus:

☐ your GP
☐ your lover
☐ your life insurance
   company

☐ your family
☐ your dentist
☐ your employer
☐ anyone else you choose

9   Which of the following ways of making love are safe:

☐ kissing
☐ heavy petting
☐ vaginal intercourse
   without a condom

☐ anal intercourse with a
   condom
☐ oral sex
☐ masturbation (wanking)

10   If a friend has the virus you should:

☐ stop seeing them
☐ give them all the support
   you can

☐ tell their family
☐ avoid touching them

Permission is granted to photocopy pages 78–9.

AIDS quiz – answers

1   The Human Immunodeficiency Virus (HIV) has been
    shown to be transmitted through the passing of certain
    bodily fluids from one person to another. These are blood,
    blood products, semen, vaginal and cervical secretions, and
    organ transplants. There is *no evidence* of the virus being
    passed through toilet seats; mosquitoe bites; masturbation,
    swimming in a public swimming pool; using someone
    else's toothbrush; using drugs (where needles are not
    shared); or sharing a glass.
        Tatooing, ear-piercing and going to the dentist are all
    completely safe where equipment has been properly
    sterilised. Giving blood is safe because clean needles are
    used every time. All blood for transfusion has been
    screened since 1985, so there is a close to zero chance of
    catching the virus this way. Giving first aid, including
    mouth-to-mouth resuscitation, is completely safe where
    reasonable precautions are taken to avoid ingesting
    someone else's blood. Someone with bad cuts or sore or
    bleeding gums should avoid giving mouth-to-mouth
    resuscitation. Similarly, no one has been shown to have
    caught the HIV virus through love bites or kissing. It is
    advisable not to share razors or sex toys such as vibrators.
        Information changes all the time. To keep up to date
    contact the Terence Higgins Trust or the National Aidsline.
2   None of these, since it is what people do, not who they are,
    that puts them at risk.
3   Nobody knows. But this is not a trivial question since it is
    often an outlet for blaming rather than mere curiosity. For
    example, the idea that AIDS originates in Africa plays into
    white Western racism.
4   If you want a test you can get one from an STD (VD) clinic
    (see under VD in the telephone book). The test is not for
    AIDS, but it will tell you if your body has been exposed to
    the HIV virus. To be absolutely sure of a negative (all-
    clear) result you will need to have another test 3–4 months
    later since the virus may take this amount of time to
    incubate. There are lots of pros and cons to having a test
    and it needs to be thought about carefully. (See the
    Terence Higgins Trust leaflets on testing.)
5   They are infectious and therefore need to ensure that they
    do not pass the virus on, which can be done by practising
    safer sex and not sharing needles. They are not 'dangerous'
    by virtue of having the virus itself. Pregnancy puts a strain
    on the body's defences and so can be a danger to women

who are HIV positive and showing symptoms of illness. Pregnancy does not appear to affect HIV positive women who are not ill, nor are the babies of such women automatically born HIV+. Figures for the life expectancy for those with HIV or with AIDS change all the time. However, it is clear that much can be done by an individual to stay healthy and in a positive frame of mind.

6   All of these could be symptoms of AIDS. On the other hand, they could be symptoms of another viral infection, too.

7   None of these, necessarily. A person should certainly not be isolated and alone when they are ill. It is a time when they will need all the help they can get. They may have to stop work if they become too ill and they may not feel like having sex. However, as long as they practise safer sex they will not spread the virus. Most people with AIDS will eventually die from it, but due to new treatments and better understanding of the syndrome, more PWAs (persons with AIDS) are living longer and with a better quality of life.

8   It's up to you and who you trust. You may want to confide in people and get their support to ensure that you do not pass on the infection. On the other hand, people's fear may lead them to discriminate against you. People have been sacked for being HIV positive and currently, life insurance companies will not insure you if you have taken a test, whether you are positive or not.

9   Kissing, wanking and heavy petting are not risky in terms of passing on or catching the virus. Anal and vaginal intercourse with a condom, lubricant (water based) and spermicide containing Nonoxynol 9 will cut down – though not eliminate – the risk considerably. Oral sex has a low to medium risk.

10   They will almost certainly need support, understanding and comforting including touching. It must be their decision to tell their family.

Negotiating safer sex – what would you: feel? say? do?

1 You meet someone new at a party. They invite you back to their place. How would you feel? What would you do?

2 You meet someone at a club/disco who you know has had several relationships recently. At the end of the night they invite you back to their place. How would you feel? What would you do?

3 You've met someone you fancy and gone back to their house. It's getting late and you are expecting that you will have sex with them. They say 'Before we go any further, we need to talk about sex.' How would you feel? What would you do?

4 You are in bed with a partner and both of you are getting excited when they say 'Hold on. I don't want to have intercourse.' How would you feel? What would you do?

5 You are in bed with a partner, when it occurs to you that maybe you had better use a condom. What would you say? What would you do?

6 You are going to be having sex with someone you've just met. As you are starting to get undressed they say, 'Oh by the way – I never use condoms. They just get in the way.' How would you feel? What would you do?

7 You've been going out with someone for quite a long time. One night they say, 'I think we'd better use a condom – don't you?' How would you feel? What would you say?

8 You are about to go to bed with someone and they say, 'Look, I don't want to have intercourse but I do have lots of other interesting suggestions.' How would you feel? What would you do?

9　You have just been to the STD clinic and been told that you have a non-fatal but infectious STD, such as genital warts. The next night you meet someone you really fancy and it looks like you are going to have sex. What would you do? What would you say?

10　You had sex with someone you think might be infected with HIV and decide to have a test. You get an 'all-clear' result. How would you feel? What would you do?

11　You are going out with someone and after a couple of weeks they tell that they have been tested and they are all clear. How would you feel? What would you do?

12　A mate of yours tells you 'Once you've had the test and you're clear you're OK. You can get on with enjoying yourself.' What would you think?

Match but don't catch - STDs and their symptoms

Gonorrhoea	Symptoms	pain when peeing, yellow discharge from penis or anus often no symptoms for a woman
	Caught by	sexual intercourse
Syphilis	Symptoms	4 stages: painless sores/spots on sex organs; skin rash which goes eventually; heart, lungs, brain attacked over many years; paralysis, blindness, madness, death
	Caught by	sexual intercourse
Thrush	Symptoms	thick white discharge (like cottage cheese), pain on peeing, itching can get infected under foreskin

Thrush	Caught by	can be passed on from a partner. Yeast which causes thrush grows naturally in the vagina and when there is an imbalance can arise spontaneously
Chlamydia	Symptoms	discharge, soreness, pain on peeing rarely get symptoms but can carry the infection
	Caught by	sexual intercourse, but not always
NSU (Non-Specific Urethritis	Symptoms	discharge, pain on peeing
	Caught by	sexual intercourse but not always
Lice	Symptoms	itching around pubic and other hairy parts of body
	Caught by	close physical contact, e.g. sex, but also from towels, beds, etc.
Scabies	Symptoms	itching skin between fingers, around waist, under armpits
	Caught by	close physical contact, e.g. sex, but also from towels, beds, holding hands
Genital herpes	Symptoms	painful sores on sex organs
	Caught by	sexual contact
Genital warts	Symptoms	warts on/near sex organs
	Caught by	usually from sexual contact
Cystitis	Symptoms	pain on peeing, need to pee often
	Caught by	many causes but often appears after intercourse
Foreskin infection	Symptoms	red, swollen, itching pus around foreskin of penis
	Caught by	not cleaning properly

What is sexuality?

A session

'What is sex?' says Dave, the supervisor, reading out the quiz I've handed out. 'This should be interesting.'

'Seems obvious to me,' says Tony with resignation.

I give them some time to go through the questions. There is much conferring, muttering and giggles. Afterwards we go through it together.

'Men always want sex,' I say. 'What do you think.'

'That's crap,' says Tony seriously. 'No one always wants sex.' Someone tries to wind him up with a barbed comment but he does not respond. 'Sometimes you just don't fancy it.' Some of the others nod in agreement.

'What about blokes who rape,' someone says, 'and nonces. They want it all the time.'

'Yeah, dirty old men.' Several of them argue that men who rape are sexually frustrated, nutters. I tell them that the majority of rapists are known to their victims, are friends, relatives or colleagues.

In most groups young men are fairly universal in condemning rapists. Yet it is also common for someone to make a 'jokey' remark about rape or to talk about sex in such a way that they might as well be describing rape. Working with young men's attitudes to rape means confronting their deeply held attitudes and feelings towards women in general. Running a session specifically on rape or sexual harrassment seems to make young men incredibly defensive, and they stick to the attitude that considers rapists to be 'nutters' and nothing to do with us. Rather more successful has been to consistently pick up on the casual comments and to include rape as part of a discussion on sexuality and relationships between men and women. Encouraging young men to question the attitudes and feelings they have about women needs to go hand in hand with presenting alternatives, i.e. that men can be sexual without being predators.

Tony changes the subject. 'Well, those nonces who rape kids should be castrated, that's well out of order. I just can't understand it.' All agree vehemently, expressing their disgust for child abusers. I try to get them to say why they think they do it. They don't take up the question. 'Chop their balls off,' is all anyone will say.

There is a similar reluctance to think about what sexual abuse is really about. The connections between abuse and 'normal' male sexuality don't get made. As with rape, it is very hard for young men to understand and accept sexual abuse as a function of the way men are brought up to be sexual when there are no alternative models of sexuality on offer. The best way forward is to start talking about how men can be sexual without exploiting others.

It is also worth remembering that it is quite possible that in any group, there may be a young man who has been involved as perpetrator or victim in some form of sexual abuse. Sensitivity is required in dealing with this issue. There needs to be room for it to be talked about, for connections to be made and awareness increased, but it is not the place to deal with an individual's deeper feelings of distress. Be prepared to make yourself available after the session ends, in case anyone wants to approach you privately.

The discussion continues, with Tony saying, 'Anyway, I reckon women want it much more than blokes.' More nods of agreement. They all look world weary.

Another question comes up about whether a large penis is important. 'It's not how big it is, it's what you do with it, isn't it?' says Tony, appealing to me for confirmation. A conversation follows about what makes a good lover. There is much talk of 'knowing positions', 'moving right' (Tony stands up and swings his hips), 'Keeping going all night long', and 'pleasing a woman'. I say that it all sounds like hard work, rather than pleasure.

Performance rears it head yet again. In adolescence the pressure to 'be a man', sexually, is enormous. If it's not having a bigger dick than the next man, then it's being able to use it better. Sexual pleasure is had by doing something to someone else. Sex becomes a competitive sport like any other. I try to take the pressure off by joking and getting them to think about what actually happens between them and someone else rather than the fantasy.

I move on to another question. 'What's the difference between a man's orgasm and a woman's? They look blank. 'Remember we talked about what an orgasm was like? What happens for a woman?' Still they look blank. I discuss sexual response in men and women.

Gary interrupts me to say, 'Oh yeah, women can have one after another, can't they?'

'It's not fair, is it', says Tony with disappointment.

'What do you think a woman feels?' They still look blank. 'Well, how would you find out?'

'Ask her I suppose,' says Chris hesitantly, as if he's making a

fool of himself. I ask if they've ever talked to girls about sex.
They say yeah but not like that, that it would be too
embarrassing to ask.

These conversations show that it is very difficult to talk about
how we experience sex, what our feelings are, and whether it is
the same for men and women, straight or gay. Pleasure is one
of the main – not the only – components of our sexuality, yet as
men we rarely reveal what our experience is, even to our sexual
partners. We are inarticulate about our sexual feelings. This can
be a problem not only because it makes us poor commun-
icators, especially when things go wrong, but also because it is
these feelings that need to be examined if we are to start
dealing with the most problematic aspects of male sexuality –
rape, child abuse, pornography.

We finish the quiz and I bring out my collection of picture
cards (magazine photos, postcards, etc) and suggest we move
on to looking at what desire is. Why do we fancy some people
and not others? What makes someone attractive? I go through
the cards, starting with pictures of women first. I ask why they
pick out some as attractive and not others.

'It's obvious, innit,' says someone. 'Look at them!' We talk
about what is most important – looks, money, personality. There
is some disagreement. I ask if they expect to go out with
women who look like these pictures.

'That's different. You don't expect a girl to look like a model.'

'I do,' says Tony. 'I'm not settling for anything less.'

'You've got a long wait then, haven't you,' says Chris.

The conversation/argument carries on about the best
approach to life – be 'realistic' or don't settle for less.

Concerns about our attraction to others, our attractiveness
and our expectations of sexual partners are usually kept to
ourselves. However, we all spend a lot of time, particularly in
adolescence, thinking about these issues, especially when things
go wrong. In our society, so much is influenced by images from
films, TV and newspapers that conflicts with what we
experience as individuals. Men's sexuality, in particular, is built
around fantasy, cutting us off from our real selves.

The session continues. I bring out some pictures of men and
ask the group to consider whether they are attractive or not.
'Men? Get lost!'

'I'm only asking if you think they are attractive or not,' I say.

'How would we know, we're not queers are we!' says Chris,
looking round him for support. The defences have come up and
the atmosphere changes immediately. I suggest that they
consider whether women would find them attractive and then

think about whether there is anything they admire or respect about the men. Several concede to admiring Clint Eastwood because 'he won't let himself be pushed around', and Don Johnson from 'Miami Vice' because he's 'cool'. They agree with each other that most film stars are attractive just because they are rich and famous. I ask if gay men would find any of these men attractive.

'No use asking us,' says Chris emphatically again.

'Just think about it,' I say. 'What makes a man attractive to other men? Is it the same things that women find attractive in men?'

One or two venture the opinion that it might be the same until Tony intervenes. 'I don't understand. Why do they do it?'

''Cos they're sick,' says Chris.

I focus my attention on Tony who seems to want to understand. 'Why do you fancy women?'

'It's nature, isn't it.'

'Well what's unnatural about men fancying other men?'

'That's obvious. They can't have babies, can they?' he says, laughing and looking round for acknowledgement from the others.

'So you have sex just to have babies?'

'No but . . .'

'They should be shot,' says Chris, looking furious, arms folded, staring at the wall ahead. The others are shuffling their feet. I ask them what they think. Silence.

In almost every single session I've ever run someone has made some kind of derogatory remark about gay men or lesbians. It's not surprising since there is nothing more certain to bring up men's fear of homosexuality than being with other men. For a man to be sexual with another man is a very powerful example of closeness. The oppression of gay men stems from this fear. Consequently a strategy for dealing with this fear must involve men getting closer to one another. This will help to defuse the prejudice against gay men but also be a major benefit to heterosexual men as well.

Lesbianism threatens men's view of how the world should operate. Men's reaction to women who don't need them sexually, and in some cases don't need them at all, can vary from hatred, to disbelief or even voyeurism. These attitudes will continue as long as men view women as objects who exist for the gratification of their sexual (and other) needs.

Looking at sexuality more openly should help men to realise that there are no rules of absolute 'normalness', and that gay men and lesbians are not alien species.

This full session has had a difficult ending. I ask if anyone wants to add anything or ask any questions. They don't. I hang around talking to Dave, the supervisor.

Information

Sexual response in men and women; background reading on sexuality, homosexuality, rape, sexual abuse and porn.

Reading

Basic

J. Cousins, *Make It Happy*
R. Bell *et al.*, *Changing Bodies, Changing Lives*
B. Zilbergeld, *Men And Sex*
L. Trenchard & H. Warren, *Something To Tell You*

Further

P. Gordon & L. Mitchell, *Safer Sex: A New Look at Sexual Pleasure*
A. Dickson, *The Mirror Within*
Shere Hite, *The Hite Report On Male Sexuality*
A. Metcalf & M. Humphries (eds.), *The Sexuality Of Men*
E. White, *A Boy's Own Story*

Resources

1   'True Romance' – video

2   'Framed Youth' – video

3   What is sex? – quiz on pleasure and sexual response

Aims

To raise issues about sexual behaviour and sexual response.

How to use

Get individuals to fill in and then go through the answers in the group.

This quiz is set out on page 94.

4   Sexuality means . . .?

Aims

To highlight the range of sexual expression, gay and lesbian as well as heterosexual, and the place of sexuality in our lives.

How to use

Transfer questions on to cards and get individuals to read one out. Encourage group discussion.

The questions are set out on page 95.

5   Just a bit of a laugh . . .?

Aims

To raise issues about appropriate/inappropriate sexual behaviour around rape, sexual harrassment, sexual exploitation and abuse.

How to use

Transfer statements on to cards. Get the group to divide into three areas of the room according to their views, as to whether each statement is 'acceptable', 'unacceptable', or 'don't know'. Then members of each 'viewpoint' try to convince members of other two groups to join them. Give a few minutes to each statement, then move on. Act as referee.

The statements are set out on page 96.

6   Harmless fun or fun-less harm? Pornography – a questionnaire

Aims

To encourage discussion about what we feel, think and believe about porn.

How to use

Get individuals to fill in the questionnaire and then go through the answers in the group.

The questionnaire is set out on page 97.

7 Problem page

Aims

To acknowledge the fact that men do have problems; to help make young men aware that they have the capacity to help others.

How to use

You will need a collection of 'problem letters' either collected from magazines or made up by yourself. Pick or compose problems that are fairly typical to men. Read out the letter and encourage the group to say both how they feel about the writer's problems and what they think he should do.

8 Attraction – picture cards

Aims

To encourage discussion and questioning of the assumptions made about what makes someone 'attractive'. Are there different standards for men and women? Do personal qualities count as much as physical attributes? Why are famous people assumed to be more attractive than 'ordinary' people. Are lesbians and gay men attracted by the same kinds of qualities as heterosexual men and women? How does seeing someone as a 'hero' fit into this?

How to use

Collect some pictures – postcards, magazine cuttings of men and women, both famous and 'ordinary'. Get the group to evaluate them in terms of how 'attractive', they are, for both the women and the men. Ask what it is that makes them attractive. Don't define 'attractive' at the beginning, just ask for their first reaction. Then start to talk about what 'attractive' means, about what makes someone 'attractive'.

Here are some questions you might want to ask:

- What makes a woman attractive to men?
- What makes a woman attractive to other women?
- What makes a man attractive to women?
- What makes a man attractive to other men?
- Even if we are not sexually attracted to other men, are there things about them that we admire or respect?
- Do we try to mould ourselves in the image of certain men – either famous men or men we know – to make ourselves more attractive?
- What is the difference between fancying someone (finding them attractive) and liking them?
- What is the difference between fancying someone and loving them?
- What is the difference between liking someone and loving them?

9   Brainstorm – the 'perfect man' & the 'perfect woman'

Aims

See above.

How to use

Ask the group to brainstorm all the qualities that make the 'perfect man' and 'perfect woman' in terms of their attractiveness.

Here are some follow-up questions you might want to ask.

- What happens to those of use who do not match up to this ideal of perfection? (Anybody here think they match up to it?)
- How influenced are we by these images of perfect men and women?
- How can we tell if we are attractive or not?
- Name three things about yourself that others would find attractive.

10   What the papers say – homosexuality

Aims

To raise awareness of the way lesbians and gay men are represented in the media and thus to show how they create and reinforce prejudice and stereotyping; to counter this information with a more accurate representation of the lives of lesbians and gay men.

How to use

Collect a selection of stories from newspapers and magazines which feature lesbians or gay men. Check out what people believe. Correct any misinformation that comes up. Perhaps show clippings from the gay press to illustrate the 'normality' of non-heterosexual lifestyles. Compare with the way heterosexual relationships are portrayed as 'everyday' and 'normal'.

Compare the treatment of gay men and lesbians by the newspapers with that of other groups or activities known and familiar to the young men, e.g. the way the media handle stories about drugs and young people or football and violence. This may help to illustrate the way the press can distort, misrepresent and sensationalise.

11   What the papers say – page 3, advertising and porn

Aims

To illustrate the connections between images of women in porn with the more 'acceptable' images of women used in the popular media.

How to use

Collect clippings from newspapers (page 3) and magazines (adverts) which use women to sell a product.

- Can you see any similarity in the images with those used in pornography?
- Why do advertisers and newspapers feel they need to use women like this to sell their product?
- Are men used in this way?
- What do these images say?

What is sex? Quiz on pleasure and sexual response

		T	F
1	Sex is . . .		
	just good fun	☐	☐
	dirty	☐	☐
	for married couples only	☐	☐
	best when you are in love	☐	☐
	something you shouldn't talk about	☐	☐
	the same thing as intercourse	☐	☐
	a good way to sell newspapers	☐	☐
2	Men always want sex.	☐	☐
3	Men want sex more than women.	☐	☐
4	A man needs a big penis to be a good lover.	☐	☐
5	A woman needs big breasts to be a good lover.	☐	☐
6	Women can suffer from 'premature ejaculation' (coming too soon).	☐	☐
7	A woman's orgasm is the same as a man's.	☐	☐
8	Only boys can masturbate.	☐	☐
9	Gay men and lesbians enjoy sex in the same way as straight (heterosexual) men and women.	☐	☐
10	A man should always take the lead in sex.	☐	☐

Sexuality means

Why do people have sex?

At what age do we first have sexual feelings? When do people stop being interested in sex?

Do you think it's possible to masturbate too much?

How would you react if a member of your family or a friend told you they were lesbian or gay?

Does everyone have sexual feelings? What about those who are celibate (people who choose not to have sexual relationships)?

Would you go out with someone you didn't like if you thought you could have sex with them?

Do you think it's best to

- find one sexual partner for life
- move from one partner to another
- have several at a time?

At what age do people know whether they are gay, straight or bisexual?

Why is it almost always men who use pornography?

Is there something wrong with men who use prostitutes?

Put in order of importance: family, sport, sex, money, friends, a job.

1 . . . .   2 . . . .

3 . . . .   4 . . . .

5 . . . .   6 . . . .

Just a bit of a laugh . . .?

A woman is walking past a building site. Several men whistle and shout at her.

A man at work making jokes about the size of a woman colleague's breasts.

A man touching up a woman in a crowded underground train.

A group of young men staring at two women sitting together in a pub.

A husband insisting that his wife has sex with him because it's 'his right'.

A boy making a 'heavy breathing' phone call to a girl in his class for a joke.

A father showing his son his porn magazines.

A father showing his daughter his porn magazines.

A young boy sitting on his grandfather's knee. Grandfather strokes his hair.

A judge at a trial saying that a man's rape of his stepdaughter was 'understandable' because his wife was pregnant at the time and was not interested in sex.

A man raping a prostitute.

Harmless fun or fun-less harm . . . Pornography – a questionnaire

		Agree	Disagree
1	Pornography is harmless – it's just a bit of fun.	☐	☐
2	Porn is used only by those men who are sexually frustrated.	☐	☐
3	Porn is dangerous because it can turn men into rapists.	☐	☐
4	Porn is a good way to learn about sex.	☐	☐
5	Some porn is all right but some of it goes too far	☐	☐
6	Porn in a way for a few people to make easy money out of gullible men.	☐	☐
7	Page three is a kind of porn.	☐	☐
8	Looking at porn excites me but also makes me feel guilty.	☐	☐
9	I have never and would never look at porn	☐	☐
10	Porn makes women into sex objects and exploits them.	☐	☐
11	Watching blue movies is a laugh.	☐	☐
12	Women like porn as much as men.	☐	☐
13	Porn is dangerous because it gives you the wrong idea about real-life relationships.	☐	☐
14	What happens in blue movies is nothing like real life. It's just a fantasy and so does not affect anyone.	☐	☐

Permission is granted to photocopy this page.

Sexism, men and women

A session

The credits role, the music plays and the feet start to shuffle.
There is a silence.

'Is that it then?' says Chris. 'Isn't there any more?'

'Did you like it then?' I ask.

'It was crap,' he replies.

'It was all right,' says Errol simultaneously, then stops
realising his 'mistake'.

We've been watching 'Danny's Big Night', a half hour film
which focuses on the relationship between one young man, his
girlfriend and a group of his male friends. It's always like this
after watching a video. No one knows quite what to do. Groups
always seem to react like a cinema audience. First there is quiet,
then a few jokes, then they want to go straight home. At this
point I feel I've got to be on my toes, be interested, cheerful,
enthusiastic and ask questions until somebody takes a bite.

'What did you think of Danny, then?' I ask them. 'Queer!', 'A
right wanker!' A discussion starts about how Danny should
have done this or that, how he was too 'soft' with his girlfriend,
how they wouldn't have stood for it. I try to focus their
attention on specific incidents in the film. What would you have
done, thought, felt when Danny . . .? They start arguing about
whether the girlfriend was a 'slag' or not for carrying
contraceptives.

Not for the first time men's sexism rears its head. An
understanding of it is important in all our work with young
men. Sexism limits women's access to power, resources and the
means to express all aspects of their personality. It affects
women in all aspects of their lives: through violence, sexual
harrassment and rape, through the fight for equal pay and
childcare facilities, through their representation in the media or
in pornography. In sexual relationships it is just as entrenched,
made evident in these young men's belief that women who
carry contraceptives have many partners and that those who
have many partners are 'slags'.

One young man ventures the opinion that girls should be
able to sleep with whoever they like and Errol agrees. The three
loudest group members attack him furiously for this. The first
boy goes quiet, but Errol holds out with everyone rounding on
him now. He's breaking two rules: first, that of being 'different',
and second, that of being sympathetic towards women. I try to
take the heat off him by asking the others why it's all right for

them to sleep around but not women. Blokes get called 'studs' but women 'slags'. Why? 'It's different for blokes.' Why? 'That's just how it is. They're just slags, that's all.' The defences come up and a sullen silence follows.

For many men sexism just isn't seen as a problem. Many men believe that sexism is just a reflection of the natural order of things – it just 'is'. It is important that we become aware of the effects sexism can have on women's lives. These effects are not just trivial or silly or the moanings of a 'minority', but they can be fundamentally detrimental to the quality of women's lives, and at their most extreme, are life-threatening. This means men should spend time looking at the way we as men behave towards women and at the attitudes, feelings and beliefs we have about them. Obviously, this isn't going to be easy, and this group's reaction is a fairly typical one – defensiveness and denial.

I try to get the conversation going again. At one point Danny says, 'You've got to look after her, show her who's boss.' 'Do you think girls need looking after?' Silence.

This is a crucial point in the session. There is defensiveness and a hint of hostility. They may start to assume now that I'm not 'on their side' and that therefore I'm against them. It's times like this when I need to be quite clear that there is a difference between their true selves and how they have been conditioned to feel and behave. This is not always easy. I have come up against some of men's most deep-rooted assumptions.

Why is sexism to entrenched? The obvious answer is that it is in men's interest to perpetuate this oppression, and certainly economically, in terms of retaining 'power-over', this is true. But it is also because men are frightened of women and what they represent, in this case women's sexuality – qualities men are conditioned 'out of' – like vulnerability, sensitivity, sensuality, an ability to be intimate.

I try to catch someone's eye, one of the quieter ones, and engage them with a question. It's not working. Dave, the supervisor, comes to the rescue.

'I think my wife looks after me much more than the other way round.'

'Well, that's a woman's job, isn't it – to look after men,' says one boy.

'Sexist,' retorts another, with a grin on his face.

'It's a man's job to look after a woman, but it's a woman's job to look after a man?' I ask.

A confused and energetic discussion ensues about what women are expected to do for men and men for women. There are many shades of opinion but the conversations begins to focus on what women are expected to do for them, some of the group vying with each other to be the most outrageously sexist.

This is another example of the 'that's just the way it is' school of thought about men and women. We are born 'male' and 'female', but we learn to be 'men' and 'women'. Our sex is determined in pregnancy and our gender is learned as we grow. This learning means being pushed into certain 'roles' – housewife, mother, breadwinner, hard-man, temptress, ladies-man, family man. We come to identify with these to such an extent that we feel that they are 'just how it is'. Unfortunately, these roles are often very limited and they fail to meet our need to express all aspects of our personalities. Both men and women are restricted in this way, but men's roles usually involve more access to power, resources and status and the means to self-determination. Stereotyping is another way of describing this process where a person's individuality is replaced by a set of assumptions.

I gratefully accept the group's new-found enthusiasm and decide to develop the discussion further. I write 'MEN' on one sheet of paper and 'WOMEN' on another. I invite them to describe the differences. 'They've got tits,' says one boy and he gets a few giggles. I tell him I'm glad he's been paying attention during the anatomy session. 'Be serious', says Tony returning to his role as self-appointed 'mature-man' of the group. I ask them to try to describe women without insults and without mentioning parts of their body. Silence returns. They don't seem to understand what I'm getting at, but it starts to get moving when Dave, the supervisor, and I throw in a few suggestions. Some of the characteristics end up being put on both lists because 'everyone's like that'. After a while they dry up. I ask whether they personally would feel happy being described by the words on the male list. Most nod in agreement, although a couple say that they don't think men are really as 'confident' as they make out. The rest think it's pretty accurate. I turn to the 'women' list and ask them what it would be like if I called them, for example, 'gentle'. A few protest strongly but others say it would be a compliment. 'What about "beautiful",' I say. 'I'd smash you in the face if you called me that,' says one. 'Sensitive?' ('Depends'). 'Sexy?' ('No way!')

What have men to gain by letting go of sexism? Themselves. Although men can benefit by perpetuating sexism they also lose out in their ability to show their true selves. As with other oppressions, cracks and contradictions continually appear which provide opportunities for change. Men's need for satisfying

sexual and emotional relationships is one such area. By letting
go of the stereotyped sex roles which limit their natural desire
to be close, they could learn to communicate well with other
men, women and children. Younger men, like those in this
group, have less distance between them and the 'feminine' or
childlike qualities older men have long ago put behind them.
They try desperately to 'prove' they are men because they lack
guidance on what this really means. Talking about the
limitations they must experience and being offered the
possibility of alternatives might help free them from the need to
limit women's role. Ironically, how men can let go of their sexist
views is by more fully becoming men.

In the group, we continue for a while to talk about whether
these stereotyped sex roles are a good thing or not. Do they get
in the way? Their interest starts to wane and I add further to
their confusion by saying that next session we will be looking at
what being a man is all about. 'I can tell you all about that,' says
Tony as he swaggers out of the room.

Information

Some background reading and thinking about sexism.

Reading

Basic

H. Dixon & G. Mullinar (eds.), *Taught Not Caught* (pages 63–5)
B. Zilbergeld, *Men And Sex*
S. Askew & C. Ross, *Boy's Don't Cry*

Further

Judith Arcana, *Every Mother's Son*
H. Slavin (ed.), *Greater Expectations*
S. Hemmings, *Girls Are Powerful*

Resources

1 'True Romance' – video

2 'Danny's Big Night' – video

3 What the papers say . . . women

Aim

To show how the media reinforces stereotypes.

How to use

- Make a selection of adverts from magazines. What do these say about the roles of women and kind of people they are expected to be?
- Take a selection of newspapers. How many women feature in articles about politics, sport, finance and business and 'human interest'. What does this say about women? Do the papers have a 'Woman's Page'? What kind of thing does it feature? Why are there not separate 'Man's Pages'?
- Look at the way women are described in newspaper stories. How often does it say 'blond, attractive 26 year old . . .' etc? Are men ever described like this, i.e. with reference to their attractiveness, or age?

4   Role reversal

Aims

To show both how stereotyping is rooted in our language, and to have a bit of fun.

How to use

For this exercise you need to get hold of a copy of *Taught Not Caught* (see page 122). On pages 63–5 there is a short playlet. Copy it out and get some volunteers to read it out loud. Discuss.

In advance prepare another set of scripts. This time try taking the scene and reversing all the gender references, e.g. 'How's the Mrs?' becomes 'How's the Mister?' etc. Now get volunteers to read this version out loud, acting the parts as women. Prepare for much giggling and confusion. Discuss. Why does all this seem so ridiculous? If it's ridiculous for us as men to be talked about like this, then how does it feel for women to have to put up with this all the time?

5   Thinking about . . . oppression

Aims

To evoke the experiences we will all have had of times
when we felt powerless or humiliated or treated unfairly; to
then make a connection with the way sexism affects
women.

How to use

Ask the group to think of a time when they remember
feeling humiliated, treated unfairly or made fun of yet felt
powerless to do anything about it. Get them to describe
what it was like. Discuss in the group and suggest that this
is how women often feel in the face of sexism and
discrimination.
     If used carefully and subtly this can be a good way to get
young men to make the connection between various forms
of oppression. All of them will have experienced some
form of this as children in relation to adults. Young black
men, those of minority religions, young gay men, and
young disabled men will have an even more extensive
experience of this.

6   Brainstorm 'men' and 'women'

Aim

To assess awareness and assumptions about gender roles
and the differences between men and women.

How to use

Get the group to shout out their first thoughts, write these
down without censoring the ideas, then discuss.

7   On the one hand, on the other hand . . . men and women

Aims

To raise awareness about the effects of gender roles and
how we feel about them.

How to use

Brainstorm –

- 'The advantages of being a man'
- 'The disadvantages of being a man'
- 'The advantages of being a woman'
- 'The disadvantages of being a woman'

Either do this in a large group or divide into four sub-groups with one question each. You could use the follow-up questions from the 'Stereotypes' exercises to further discussion.

Note: I have found in doing this exercise that young (and adult) men will tend to define the advantages of being a man in terms of their not being women. This is an important point which highlights men's lack of a positive sense of what male identity is, preferring to see it as 'not-woman'. This is similar to white people's (who also hold power) lack of awareness of their whiteness.

8   Stereotypes

Aim

To raise awareness of stereotyping and the way men and women are pressured into sex roles.

How to use

Make the lists of jobs, qualities and behaviours into cards. Go through them asking the group which are acceptable for women, which for men and which for both. Encourage questioning of why this is so. Add your own ideas.

Which of the following jobs are more suitable for women, which for men?

Plumber, Prime Minister, nurse, bricklayer, doctor, lawyer, newsreader, pilot, police inspector, midwife, footballer, bishop, teacher, secretary, physiotherapist, miner, scientist, cleaner, chef, home help, journalist, sex education teacher.

Which of the following qualities are more likely to be used to describe men or women?

Gentle, clever, strong, sensitive, understanding, funny, hard, quiet, caring, assertive, vulnerable, glamorous, aggressive, beautiful, trustworthy, argumentative, quiet, emotional, lustful, fearful, selfish, sensual, arrogant, sexy, insecure, confident, lazy, single-minded, trusting, stubborn.

Which of these behaviours are more typical of men, which more typical of women?

Asking someone to dance; playing it 'cool' or hard to get; only having sex when in love; chatting someone up; making the first move to have sex; walking arm in arm with your best friend; crying when upset; getting into a fight; comforting a child who's upset; comforting a friend who's upset; doing the housework; shouting 'sexy' at someone in the street; looking after an elderly relative; worrying whether they are attractive or not.

Follow-up questions

- Are these roles a bad thing? Who benefits from these divisions?
- Do they limit us? Are there any of them that *you* feel limited by, i.e. is there anything you would like to do or be but dare not because it's a 'woman's role'?
- How do these stereotypes and roles affect our relationships? Do you expect women to act in a certain way and men in another e.g. men to be aggressive, or women to do the housework?
- What happens when someone does not act the way we expect them to? What happens if a man were to become a secretary, or a women a bricklayer? What kind of reaction would they get?
- Is it possible to change these roles and stereotypes? Have they changed in any way in your lifetime? Ten years ago if a boy wore a pink sweater he would be called a 'girl', a 'poof' etc. Now it is common for young men to wear pink and other bright colours. What changes have there been in sex roles from 10, 20, 50 100 years ago? What is acceptable now that was not before?

9   'Where men are men and women are women . . .'

Aim

To provoke thought and discussion about gender roles and about the relationships between men and women.

How to use

Transfer statements listed below on to cards. Get the group to divide into three areas of the room according to whether they 'agree', 'disagree' or 'don't know' in relation to each statement. Then members of each viewpoint try to convince members of the other two groups to join them. Give a few minutes to each statement, then move on. Act as referee.

Statements

Blue for boys and pink for girls.

Women and their friends are closer than men and their friends.

Women and men have more similarities than differences.

A man and a woman can never be 'just friends'. There is always sex involved somewhere.

You can talk to women friends in a way you can't talk to men friends.

Women are the equal of men.

Women are treated equally to men.

Adults treat girls differently to boys.

Men are more violent than women.

More is expected of boys than of girls.

All this stuff about sexism is a fuss about nothing.

Sexism, like racism, causes a lot of problems and unhappiness between people and should be got rid of as soon as possible.

Women need to be looked after by men.

Women should look after men.

Being a man

A session

'I thought we'd finish these sessions by looking at what being a man is like.' The group continue to look at the wall, at each other or at their feet. The beginnings of sessions still feel as difficult as they did seven weeks ago. I'm not sure where to start so I plunge in. 'When does a boy become a man?'

They look at me as if I've just landed from Mars. There's a short silence before Chris says smirking, 'When he's done the business.'

'Nah, any kid can do that,' says Tony. 'It's when he's mature, you know – got a family, settled down and all that sort of thing.'

'When he's 18 and can vote,' offers someone else.

'It just sort of happens,' says Brian who has been one of the 'quiet' ones. 'It creeps up on you and one day you realise you're not just a kid anymore.'

'So you reckon you're a man, do you,' says Chris, sneering.

'Not yet, no,' Brian replies quietly, holding his ground. I ask the rest of them if they feel they are boys or men. Most of them reply that they are men, 'nearly'.

What does being a man mean? The question may seem strange as men, unlike women, are not forced to become aware of their gender through being oppressed. In this society our learning about being men tends to happen unconsciously. For those from western secular cultures at least, the lack of formal rites of passage makes the transition from boyhood to manhood confusing and often difficult.

I ask them how they learned how to be men. They all seem puzzled, replying that it's 'natural' and that you don't need to learn. I turn the question round and ask what would be the most important thing they would tell their son if they ever had one. This works better.

'To look after number one.' 'Stick with his mates.' 'Don't get pushed around.' 'Get your retaliation in first.' 'Do what *you* want to do.' I say that it sounds like they expect him to have a hard time. 'That's just the way it is,' comes the reply.

Most of these young men are resigned to a life of isolation even from their best friends. As men we get taught to 'stand on our own two feet', to be independent, to hide our feelings from others. This, not surprisingly, makes relationships, particularly with other men, difficult. This gets compounded by the need to 'prove' our manhood.

I bring out the 'Statement' cards about men's behaviour to try and open up the discussion. Cards get picked in turn, read out, then discussed as to whether they are 'acceptable' or not. The first card reads 'a man hitting another man'. Everyone agrees that it's acceptable depending on the circumstances and that it happens all the time. I pursue this. I ask them when was the last time they were involved in some kind of violence. For half of them it has been in the last month. I ask if anyone wants to tell us their experiences. They *all* do. One after another there are stories of fights between individuals, in gangs, at parties, on the streets, in pubs and clubs. Few were regarded as 'serious' since no one was badly hurt, and most seem to be brief encounters. I asked if it bothered them that violence seemed to be so common.

'Like I said, that's the way it is. You've got to be able to look after yourself,' says Chris, 'otherwise you get pushed around like Brian here'. Brian says nothing.

'Maybe he doesn't like fighting,' I say. 'I used to avoid it at all costs!'

'Yeah, half the time it's all front,' says Tony, 'all mouth and no trousers.'

Men's violence springs from the fear and isolation we learn as we grow up. Much of men's culture is rooted in violence: in war, in guns, gangs and gansters. Being a man means being 'tougher than the rest', and this applies to the boardroom as much as it does to the street or the boxing ring. Across race, class and cultures men share a world where violence – actual or symbolic – is the norm. For young men this atmosphere of violence is an ever-present factor in their lives from the playground bully or conflict with the police to the Rambo videos watched at home.

The session continues. Someone picks out another card which reads: 'Two men walking down the street arm in arm.' 'That's disgusting. They should do it in private, not in the street, man!' says Errol. Most of the others nod in agreement.

'What's wrong with it?' I ask.

'They better not come near me, that's all!'

'Why do you think they'd want to?' I ask him. 'You're assuming gay men go around jumping on other blokes.' A discussion follows about what men do and I try to correct some of the assumptions and myths about gay men.

'Anyway, you're assuming they are gay,' I say.

'They must be. You wouldn't catch me doing that,' says Errol as he puts his arm around his mate Phil and pretends to kiss him. 'Let's go for a walk, darling,' he says to him, giggling and camping it up.

'You're doing it now,' I point out to him.

'Yeah, but that's just a joke,' he says embarrassed. 'I'm just winding you up.'

'Well I think it's good you feel able to be so affectionate with him,' I say, straightfaced.

'But it's a joke!' he protests.

Tony, who has been very quiet up to now says that back home in Cyrpus men do it all the time. It doesn't mean they fancy one another. He asks Chris, who is also from a Greek-Cypriot family, for confirmation and he, likewise quiet until now, agrees. I say that in many cultures men, gay or straight, are openly affectionate with each other in public – in France, North Africa, the Mediterranean, Eastern Europe.

Clearly, men's fear of closeness with other men is at it's most acute in heterosexual men's fear of gay men. Gay men's closeness through sex – although this may not mean emotional closeness – is a powerful threat to the separation men maintain from each other. This is accentuated by the fact that, for many men, the most likely physical contact with other men is violent contact. Being in a group of men, a sex education group for example, brings fears of closeness up to the surface, and a common response to this is strong anti-gay feelings.

Another card is read out: 'A man going out with his mate's girlfriend.' This provokes a lively debate between those who say you should 'stick with your mates' and those who think men are always 'looking after number one'. I ask them if they feel they could trust their mates. There are nervous glances all round. Only Errol sticks to his view that trust for friends is all important, and he refuses to be browbeaten by the others. I encourage the others to say what it's like not being able to trust each other. The responses are the same as before: 'That's just how it is.' I tell them I think that it's really sad.

If you have learned that you are essentially on your own, that you must not show weakness to others and that you can expect violence from them, then it's not surprising that you will see these others as rivals. From the cut-throat world of executive wheeling and dealing to the 'drink you under the table' of the 'lager lout', men's lives are fuelled by competition, by the need to be one up on the next man. This, of course, also applies to relationships where, for many men, sex equals another performance. The need to prove our manhood in competition with others is an ever-present task.

It's near the end of the session now and I suggest spending the time looking back at the sessions, to make comments or ask questions. Nobody says anything and they all look a bit uncomfortable. Dave, the supervisor, says he has really enjoyed himself, learned a lot and has not had the chance to hear men talk this this before.

It is of course obviously true that not all men's experience or relationships with other men are universally negative. Despite all that I've talked about above, men do, at times in their lives, get close to other men and let the protective barriers drop. These moments often occur at times of crisis, such as bereavement, danger or the break-up of a relationship, or these moments are remembered from early days before the constrictions of 'being a man' took hold. It is likely that all of us have, at some time at least, glimpsed what it could be like if we felt able to express our true selves. Usually these positive experiences don't get paid attention to, get passed over or deliberately suppressed. Because of our isolation we don't feel able to risk being 'different'. All the more admirable was Errol's stand, for the positiveness of 'sticking with your mates', in the face of everyone else's cynicism.

'Yeah it's been all right, a laugh.' says Tony. 'Do you really get paid for doing this kind of thing then? I'd talk about sex all day long if somebody paid me.'

'You already do – and for nothing!' says Chris.

Information

See pages 124–5 for a list of background reading on men and do some thinking about your own experience.

Reading

Basic

Phillip Hodson, *Men: An Investigation into the Emotional Male*
B. Zilbergeld, *Men And Sex*
Chris Meade, *The Him Book*
Trefor Lloyd, *Work With Boys*

Further

Stuart Miller, *Men And Friendship*
Shere Hite, *The Hite Report On Male Sexuality*
Sue Askew & Carol Ross, *Boys Don't Cry*
Alan Turkie, *Know What I Mean*

Resources

1   'Danny's Big Night' – video

2   'Teenage Father' – film

3   'A Man's World' – game from the B-Team

4   B-Team posters

5   Problem page (see page 91)

6   Myths about men – a quiz

Aims

To dispel myths, prejudices and assumptions (including racism) about being a man.

How to use

Get individuals to fill in the quiz and then go through it in the group. An important part of this process is tackling ignorance, correcting misinformation and presenting counter examples.

The quiz is set out on page 112.

7   'A man's gotta do . . .' – a questionnaire

Aims

To encourage discussion and questioning of the way men are expected to act.

How to use

Get individuals to consider the statements and then ask them to say whether they find them 'acceptable' or 'unacceptable'. Then go through the responses with the group and discuss.

The questionnaire is set out on page 113.

Myths about men - a quiz

		True	False
1	Boys don't cry.	☐	☐
2	Real men don't show their feelings.	☐	☐
3	Men are no good at looking after babies.	☐	☐
4	A man needs to be 'well-built' (muscular) to be attractive.	☐	☐
5	Looking after yourself means being able to fight.	☐	☐
6	Men are naturally violent.	☐	☐
7	Asian men are not able to 'look after themselves' in a fight.	☐	☐
8	Gay men are not real men.	☐	☐
9	There are no black gay men.	☐	☐
10	A man ought to be the breadwinner in a family.	☐	☐
11	Black men have larger penises than white men.	☐	☐
12	Men don't talk to other men about their problems.	☐	☐
13	It's a man's world.	☐	☐
14	If two men love each other it must mean they are gay.	☐	☐
15	Men don't fall in love the way women do.	☐	☐
16	You've got to be 'tougher than the rest'.	☐	☐

'A Man's Gotta Do . . .' – a questionnaire

	Acceptable	Unacceptable
A 7-year-old boy crying.	☐	☐
A 17-year-old young man crying.	☐	☐
A man hitting another man.	☐	☐
A man hitting a woman.	☐	☐
Two men walking down the street arm in arm.	☐	☐
Two men kissing each other on the cheek.	☐	☐
A man talking to a friend because he's worried about a sexual problem.	☐	☐
A man refusing promotion and becoming a full-time parent instead.	☐	☐
A man calling a woman a 'cunt'.	☐	☐
A man whistling at a woman walking down the street	☐	☐
A man refusing to fight another man.	☐	☐
A man working as a secretary to a woman boss.	☐	☐
A man going out with his mate's girlfriend.	☐	☐

Permission is granted to photocopy this page.

8   When does a boy become a man . . .?

Aim

To highlight the contradictions between being young and being male.

How to use

Brainstorm 'boy' and 'man' in group and then use follow-up questions.

Follow-up questions

- When does a boy become a man?
- Are there situations when you are in a group just with men that you find uncomfortable?
- What situations when you are just with men do you like?
- How do you learn to be a man? Who teaches you?
- Name three things you like about being a man.
- Name three things you dislike about being a man.
- Why is it an insult to say to someone 'Stop acting like a kid!'
- What does it mean when someone says 'Take it like a man'?
- Why is it an insult to call someone 'a big girl' or 'an old woman'?
- If you were ever to have a son, what would be the most important thing you would teach him?
- What do you miss most (will you miss) about not being a boy any longer?

9   Heroes

Aim

To get young men thinking about the men who have influenced them, perhaps taught them how to be men.

How to use

Either brainstorm in the group or divide the group into pairs if they are willing and give them 5 minutes to talk about their heroes. These men need not be famous. They could be dads, brothers, friends, workmates.

Follow-up questions:

- What are the qualities that make these men admirable?
- How have you been influenced by them?
- Are there any similarities between these men?
- What differences are there?

10 Man to man

Aim

To raise issues about relationships between men.

How to use

Write each 'situation' on a card and get individuals in the group to read one at a time and answer the questions 'How would you feel?' and 'What would you do?' Then discuss the answers.

Situations

- You are out shopping and you meet your best mate. He puts his arm around your shoulder as you talk.
- You've just scored the last-minute winner for your side in a cup final. Your team-mates hug and kiss you.
- You arrange to go to the cinema with your girlfriend but then your mates invite you to a party.
- You've been going out with someone for a long time and are quite keen on them. One day you spot them sitting in a cafe with your best mate.
- You have an arrangement to go out with your best mate. Someone you met at a party and who you fancy rings up and invites you out.
- You are out for a quiet drink with your girlfriend when you bump into a group of your mates in a pub.
- You are out driving with your mates. At a set of traffic lights they try to persuade you to have a 'burn-up' (a race) with another car.
- You are out with a group of mates. One of them gets drunk and starts an argument with another group of blokes.
- A good friend comes to your house late one night having had an argument with his parents. He is upset and crying.
- You are with a group of mates and they start to pick on your best friend, taking the piss and winding him up.

Appendix - Exercises for Workers

One of the main aims of this book is to encourage those who work with young people that they, not just the so-called 'experts', can provide sex education and guidance to young people. Positive relationships with young men, rather than an encyclopaedic knowledge of sex, are the key to good practice. An important part of developing such relationships is a healthy degree of awareness and acceptance of *ourselves* as sexual beings.

This doesn't mean that you should wait until you feel that you are well and truly 'sorted-out' sex-wise before daring to attempt any work with young men. Your advance preparation should certainly include some time spent considering the sexual aspects of your own life, but this can and should also be done as you go along. (If you think you are *already* fairly well 'sorted out', then it is still a good idea to allow time as the work proceeds to reflect on how it is affecting you personally.)

The exercises set out below are divided into two types, those to be done on your own and those to be done with a colleague, friend or in a group. It is important to try some of the latter even if at first they may feel more threatening. One of the key aspects of men's learning around sex is our isolation, and talking with one or more other men helps to break this down. The exercises cover the different aspects of our experience: our thinking, our feelings, our bodies and our values.

What follows is a selection of exercises, not a comprehensive list. I have taken these either from courses I have been on or books I have read. Try a few things out. For those of you who are interested in doing some further work on your own self-development, I have listed the books and a few organisations which offer courses either on sexuality or for men. Have fun!

With colleagues and friends

Questionnaire – men learning about sex

Have a go at the questionnaire on pages 18–25. You could try this on your own and then go through it with a friend or colleague.

New Grapevine Game (see page 127)

Try playing it in a support group or with colleagues. Failing that, go through the questions on your own. If you are going to use this with young men you should definitely have tried it yourself beforehand.

Brainstorming

This is a simple exercise for two or more people. Just throw out everything that comes up: assumptions, prejudices, fears, confusions, etc. Try 'sex', 'relationships', 'sexuality', 'love', etc.

Quizzes, agree/disagree cards, situation cards

Try some of the questionnaires, quizzes and games in the resources sections on your own, with a colleague or friend, or in a support group.

Listening exercises with a colleague or friend

These are some things to try with someone else, either a friend or someone you are working with. The aim is to give you the opportunity to talk and be listened to without being judged. Pick one of the topics below and spend 5 minutes talking about it. The listener should pay attention without saying anything, attempting to intervene, asking questions or offering their own opinion.

This may feel a little strange at first. Most of us will not be used to being listened to nor listening with such concentration, especially not about sex. When one person has had a turn, reverse the procedure. When you have finished, spend a few moments checking how this felt for each of you. Remember, when it's your turn, that you are in charge, and can say as little or as much as you like. Agree with your partner that whatever is said will be kept in strictest confidence.

- What you like most about sex.
- What you find most difficult about sex.

- The first sensual/sexual experience you can remember.
- The first sexual experience you can remember with another person.
- What messages do you think you picked up from your father/mother about sex?
- Can you remember any sexual experiences of any kind with someone of your own sex when you were growing up?
- The first time you masturbated.
- Describe what you like best about your own body.
- Get a condom, open the packet and tell your partner how you feel about it as you look at it and touch it.

Make up your own. The list is endless . . .

Exercises for yourself

Apart from the first, the exercises I have listed below are aimed at enhancing our awareness of our bodies. Some of the most common sexual problems men encounter arise because of our tendency to see sex simply in terms of penetration or performance and something outside ourselves, to be watched, controlled or fantasised about. In the era of AIDS this has become a dangerous liability. The following exercises attempt to encourage you to rediscover your own sensuality and will help you to build your confidence in order that you can work more effectively with young men.

Letter to self

Write a letter to yourself about 'What my life is like, sexually, at the moment'. Describe what's going well, what is difficult, anything you are worried about. Be as honest as you can.

Also try writing on the theme 'How I would like my sex life to be'. Be as detailed as you can and as ambitious as you wish.

Exploring/drawing your genitals

Take a hand mirror and have a good look at your penis and scrotum. Try and be aware of any feelings that you have as you do so. How do you feel about the size, shape and colour of all the different bits? What do different bits feel like to touch? Try making a sketch of your genitals and don't worry if it's not a Picasso.

Body exploration

This time try using a full-length mirror to explore the whole of your body. Again, what are your feelings about the different parts and as a whole?

Self portrait

Try drawing a self-portrait of your whole body but by using touch rather than vision as your guide. (You don't have to be a great artist for this. The process of getting used to touching yourself is what matters.)

Relaxation

Take some time when you will not be disturbed. Make sure the room is warm enough and then lie down on the floor. If you like you could try this exercise naked, whatever is most comfortable. Put a couple of paperback books under your head so that it is supported and on a level with the rest of your body. Take your time to slow down and become aware of your body and your breathing. When you are ready breathe in 'through' your toes and out again through them. Then move on and breathe in 'through' your feet and out and so on right up your body.

You may very will find your mind wandering off thinking you should really be doing something rather than lying here doing this silly exercise, but persevere. As men we find this kind of 'non-doing' activity pretty difficult. As you move up through your body just notice any bits that feel tense.

The point of this exercise is to let us see the constant state of activity, of get-on-to-the-next-thing-quickly type of behaviour that most of us experience.. The same principle applied to our sexual behaviour can lead to all sorts of problems.

Self massage

As with the above exercise, find a time when you will not be disturbed. Get the conditions of the room just right for you. Sit or lie down and using massage oil (baby oil or other lotion will do), start to stroke your body. Experiment with different strokes on different parts of your body. Take about 20 minutes and use the time to learn what it's like to touch your body in an unhurried but pleasurable way. By all means touch your genitals but make sure that you spend an equal time on all parts of your body. You may become sexually aroused, which is fine.

Do not masturbate during the exercise, however, but instead keep focusing on all the different ways your body is experiencing pleasure.

For many men this kind of sensual appreciation of our bodies gets ignored or undervalued in sex and we may forget that (*our*) bodies are sensual and worthy of our time and attention. You may want to apply what you have learned about yourself in your sexual activity with a partner, but remember that touching yourself in this way does not have to become a part of 'sex' and is pleasurable in its own right.

Books

The following are very accessible books which you might find useful for this kind of exercise: *Safer Sex: A New Look at Sexual Pleasure* by Peter Gordon and Louise Mitchell, and *Men and Sex* by Bernard Zilbergeld (see pages 124 and 125). There are good exercises in both on the physical/emotional aspects of sexuality.

Courses

It is of course perfectly possible to do good sex education work with young men without spending lots of time or money going on training, self-development or counselling courses, and I would re-emphasise what I said earlier about not feeling you have to 'sort yourself out' *before* starting the work. However, if you are interested in working in the area of sexuality and being a man in more depth, then I recommend below a few organisations that I have had direct experience of and have found useful. (See also pages 129–32 for others.)

- If you are interested in training specifically around sex education or more general work with young men, then write to me at the address below for details of courses I run.
  Neil Davidson
  c/o Bedford Square Press
  26 Bedford Square
  London WC1B 3HU
- Spectrum (see page 132) is an organisation based in London which runs courses on sexuality for both men and women.
- Re-evaluation Co-counselling is a method based on a theory that humans can change and heal the hurts and damaging behaviour patterns that are rooted in their early experiences. This is done through the process of learning how to counsel and be counselled. The theory and practice

are learned in classes, many of which are organised around
particular groupings, e.g. working class, middle class, black
people, lesbians, gay men, women and men. Groups are
run throughout the UK and around the world. For further
information write to me c/o the above address.

- The Brothers Programme run by David Findlay (see page
  130) for counselling and courses on the meaning of
  masculinity.
- The Family Planning Association for introductory course on
  sex education and sexuality (see page 130).

Further information

Reading

Sex education

AGGLETON, P., HORSLEY, C., WILTON, T. and WARWICK, I. *AIDS – Working with Young People*, Avert (PO Box 91, Horsham, West Sussex RH13 7YR, (0403) 864010), 1990. Contains exercises for those working with young people on the issues surrounding HIV/AIDS.

ALLEN, ISOBEL. *Education in Sex and Personal Relationships*, Policy Studies Institute, 1987. A research study which shows that sex education is wanted in schools by parents and teachers alike. Discusses influences on sexual behaviour of young people and makes recommendations.

DAVIES, MARY. *Sex Education for Young People with a Physical Disability: A Guide for Teachers*, Association to Aid the Sexual and Personal Relationships of the Disabled (SPOD), 1985. Contains information for teachers and parents on sex education.

DIXON, HILARY. *Options for Change*, Family Planning Association Education Unit, 1986. Sets out ideas for staff training for those working on personal relationships and sexuality with people with a mental handicap.

DIXON, HILARY & GORDON, PETER. *Working with Uncertainty*, Family Planning Association Education Unit, 1987. A handbook for those offering training on HIV and AIDS.

DIXON, HILARY & GUNN, MICHAEL. *Sex and the Law*, Family Planning Association Education Unit, 1987. A brief guide for staff working in the mental handicap field.

DIXON, HILARY & MULLINER, GILL (eds). *Taught Not Caught*,

Learning Development Aids, 2nd edn, 1989. Full of ideas (games, quizzes, etc.) for teaching sex education, covering such areas as: sexual decision making, puberty, contraception, STDs, relationships and communication. Also contains a good reference section.

FAMILY PLANNING ASSOCIATION EDUCATION UNIT. *Sex Education Factpack*, FPA, 1988. Useful source of information on sex education including information on sex and the law, resources plus a list of relevant agencies.

HOMANS, H., AGGLETON, P., WARWICK, I. (eds). *Learning about AIDS*, Churchill Livingstone, 1989. Contains factual information and exercises for those involved in training on the issues surrounding HIV/AIDS.

LEE, CAROL. *The Ostrich Position: Sex, Schooling and Mystification*, Unwin Paperbacks, 1986. Discusses how we are or are not taught about sex.

MASSEY, DOREEN. *School Sex Education: Why, What and How?* Family Planning Association Education Unit, 1988. A handbook for teachers looking at the aims, content and methods of sex education, integrating sex education into the curriculum, and the involvement of staff and governors.

MASSEY, DOREEN. *Teaching about HIV and AIDS*, Health Education Authority, 1988. Contains worksheets, factsheets and trigger cartoons for teachers to use with 12 to 13 years olds, 14 to 15 years olds, and 16+. Designed to help clarify information and explore attitudes and feelings.

NAM PUBLICATIONS. *The National Aids Manual*, NAM Publications (PO Box 99, London SW1 1EC, (01) 737 1846), 1989. A comprehensive information and referral resource, regularly updated. Discount available to voluntary organisations.

SLAVIN, HAZELL (ed). *Greater Expectations*, Learning Development Aids, 1986. Similar format to *Taught Not Caught* (see page 122) aimed at working with young women. Contains resource ideas that could be adapted to work with boys on the wider issues of sex and gender.

Sex and sexuality

BELL, RUTH et al. *Changing Bodies, Changing Lives*, Random House, New York, 2nd edn, 1987. Covers the 'facts' and full range of sexualities, plus quotes from young people talking about their lives.

BLANK, JOANNA. *The Playbook for Kids about Sex*, Sheba, 1982. A non-judgemental introduction to sex for young children, with illustrations.

COUSINS, JANE. *Make it Happy*, Penguin, 2nd edition, 1988. A good, basic introduction to sex and sexuality aimed at young people, but also useful for adults. Covers anatomy, contraception and STDs as well as wider issues of sexuality.

DICKSON, ANNE. *The Mirror Within*, Quartet Books, 1985. Looks at women's sexuality but also has a chapter on men.

GORDON, PETER & MITCHELL, LOUISE. *Safer Sex: A New Look at Sexual Pleasure*, Faber and Faber, 1988. Looks at how we respond positively to the challenge of AIDS and get the kind of sex life we want.

HITE, SHERE. *The Hite Report*, Dell Books, New York, 3rd edn, 1987. Massive study of women's feelings and attitudes to sex.

HITE, SHERE. *Women and Love*, Penguin, 1987. Another massive book on women's relationships and expectations.

PHILLIPS, A. & RAKUSEN, J. (eds). *The New Our Bodies Ourselves*, Penguin, 1989. A health book by and for women but useful for men since there is no equivalent.

SPENCE, CHRISTOPHER. *AIDS: Time to Reclaim our Power*, Lifestory, 1986. An essay which encourages us to respond positively to AIDS.

TRENCHARD, LORRAINE & WARREN, HUGH. *Something to Tell You*, London Gay Teenage Group, 1984. Based on research on the lives of young lesbians and gay men, this book looks at their experiences at work, at school and at home.

Men

There has been an upsurge, in recent years, of books about men. I have listed just a few of them below.

ARCANA, JUDITH. *Every Mother's Son*, the Women's Press, 1983. Looks at the role of mothers in the making of men through the author's relationship with her son.

HITE, SHERE. *The Hite Report on Male Sexuality*, Ballantine Books, New York, 1981. Many men talking about their feelings and attitudes to sex.

HODSON, PHILLIP. *Men: An Investigation into the Emotional Male*, Ariel Books (BBC Publications) 1984. Accessible and sympathetic examination of what it's like being a man.

MEADE, CHRIS. *The Him Book*, Sheffield City Libraries (Central Library, Surrey Street, Sheffield S1 1XZ), 1987. Lots of ideas for men who want to get together and look at masculinity and sexism. Also contains suggestions for working with young men.

METCALF, ANDY & HUMPHRIES, MARTIN. *The Sexuality of Men*, Pluto

Press, 1985. A collection of essays about different aspects of masculinity.

MILLER, STUART. *Men and Friendship*, Gateway Books, 1983. One man's decision to re-evaluate his friendships leads to a more general look at how men relate as friends.

TOLSON, ANDREW. *The Limits of Masculinity*, Tavistock Publications, 1977. Analyses how men are limited by restricted definitions of gender and sexuality, and how they are supported by institutions such as the family, school and work.

WALLACE, MICHELLE. *Black Macho*, J. Calder, 1979. Talks about the divisions between black men and women as effects of racism.

WHITE, E. *A Boy's Own Story*, Picador, 1983. A novel looking at growing up as a gay man.

ZILBERGELD, BERNARD. *Men and Sex*, Fontana, 1980. Aims to reassure and help men to come to terms with their own sexuality. Contains exercises. Aimed mostly at heterosexual men.

Work with boys

The National Youth Bureau has an excellent reading list containing many examples of good practice by youth workers and others. I have set out a few of the best examples below.

ASKEY, SUE & ROSS, CAROL. *Boys Don't Cry*, Open University Press, 1988. Looks at boys growing up as men and at sexism, both individual and institutional, in schools. Contains some suggestions for good practice.

LLOYD, TREFOR. *Work with Boys*, National Youth Bureau, 1985. Reasseses work with young men from the perspective of understanding them as men. Full of ideas. Looks at three examples of practice.

THOMAS CORAM PROJECT. *Camden Unemployed Young Men's Project*, available from Thomas Coram Project ((01) 267 9369), 1983. A description of a short-term piece of work with a group of young men. Charts pitfalls and successes.

Others

AGGLETON, P. *et al*. *Aids: Scientific and Social Issues*, Churchill Livingstone, 1989. Useful guide to some of current major issues surrounding AIDS.

BRAUN, DORIT. *Responding to Child Abuse: Action and Planning for Teachers and Other Professionals*, Bedford Square Press, 1988. A workbook for teachers and others on working with child sexual abuse.

CHILDREN'S LEGAL CENTRE. *Working with Young People: Legal Responsibilities and Liabilities*, Children's Legal Centre, 1984. Contains a useful section on sexuality and the law.

CHIRIMUUTA, R.C. & R.J. *Aids, Africa and Racism*, Free Association Books (26 Freegrove Road, London N7 9RG), 1989. Reassesses widely held assumptions about the spread of AIDS.

EVERYMAN PUBLICATIONS. *Working with Men*, Everyman Publications. Quarterly newsletter aimed at those working with men in the social services, probation, youth work and the health service. To be launched spring 1990.

HEMMINGS, SUSAN. *Girls Are Powerful*, Sheba, 1982. Writings on young women's lives by young women.

Where to obtain books

Compendium Books
234 Camden High Street, London NW1 8QS, (01) 267 1525

Family Planning Association Bookshop (Healthwise)
27–35 Mortimer Street, London W1N 7RJ, (01) 636 7866

National Youth Bureau
17–23 Albion Street, Leicester LE1 6GD, (0533) 471211

Films and videos

As with books there are too many videos for me to list here. I have confined myself to ones that I think work best with groups of young men.

'Am I Normal?' USA, 1979, 23 mins, colour. Distributed through Concord Films Council Ltd. Humorous presentation of some of the issues boys face on reaching puberty: wet dreams, masturbation, erections, etc. Aimed at boys reaching puberty (11–13 years).

'Coming Soon'. UK, 1987, 50 mins, colour. Distributed by Guild Sound and Vision. Five sequences are set in a coffee bar where a group of young people have a, sometimes heated, discussion about AIDS. The mood of the film changes dramatically as two 'guests' reveal themselves – one as being HIV positive and the other (a woman) as having AIDS. Features young people of different races and cultures and is set in Nottinghamshire.

'Danny's Big Night'. UK, 1985, 30 mins, colour. Distributed through the FPA Education Unit, Concord Films, Albany Video. The main aim of the film is to encourage discussion of young men's relationships with young women and with each other. Issues are brought up through the story of Danny's night out with his girlfriend. Made by a cast of black and white young actors and set in the East End of London.

'The First Days of Life' (English version). France1972, 22 mins, colour. Distributed by Boulton – Hawker Films Ltd. Concord Films Ltd, National Audio-Visual Aids Library. If you can get a decent copy and projector then this is worth it. Footage of life inside the womb as the foetus develops and ends with the birth. The mother's experience is left out, unfortunately while the film concentrates on the cosmic wonder of it all.

'Framed Youth'. UK, 1983, 50 mins, colour. Distributed by Albany Video. Young lesbians and gay men talk about their lives, sexuality, friendships, family and the oppression they face. Very bouncy and energetic but very long (there is a shorter version available). Presents strong, positive images of gay and lesbian young people. Black and white young people appear and some non-Londoners.

'Teenage Father'. USA, 1979, 30 mins, colour. Distributed through Concord Films Council Ltd. Dramatised documentary style film which through a series of interviews looks at the problems, fears and realities of a young man about to become a father. For young men 16+ who are involved in relationships with young women.

'True Romance etc.' UK, 1981, 30 mins, colour. Distributed by Concord Films and the Other Cinema. Part drama (the story of the build-up to a party) and part interviews with young people. the films explores and raises many issues about sexism, heterosexism, stereotyping and friendship. Presents very positive images of young black men and women, young lesbians and gay men. Entertaining and accessible though copies are often marred by poor sound quality. Set in London.

Other resources

The Grapevine Game. Available from Family Planning Association and National Youth Bureau (1984). A board game for 2–8 players which aims to raise issues and encourage discussion around sex and sexuality. Good non-threatening starter for a sex education group covering the 'facts' as well as attitudes and opinions.

Contraceptive Kits. Available from the Family Planning Association. A kit containing a range of contraceptives – sheaths, cap, spermicide, etc.

Male and Female. Available from the Family Planning Association. A set of 15 A4 laminated cards with illustrations of male and female sexual organs, the process of fertilisation and pregnancy.

The B-Team Posters. Available from the B-Team (see page 129). As series of six black and white posters aimed at raising issues about masculinity and sexism. Uses images of black and white men. With notes.

The Opinion Game. Available from the B-Team. A board and card game aimed at encouraging young men to talk about friendship, bodies, sex and masculinity.

Sexuality and the Mentally Handicapped. Available from the Family Planning Association and SPOD. A series of slides originally aimed at mentally handicapped young people but in fact suitable for most groups of young people. Lots of slides covering a range of subjects including bodies, puberty, parenting, STDs and contaception. Used selectively they could be very useful.

Opinions. Riverside Heath Authority & Hammersmith and Fulham Youth Service. A board game aimed at raising issues and clarifying information about HIV/AIDS.

A Man's World. The B-Team. A new boxed board game aimed at encouraging discussions on issues which affect young men's lives, such as violence, sex and relationships, work and health. Age 13+.

Useful addresses

Note on London telephone numbers

On 6 May 1990, the (01) telephone code for London will be abolished. It will be replaced by two new codes: (071) for Inner

London and (081) for outer London. Telephone numbers given below show the old (01) code, because it will still be in operation for several months after this book is published, and because the new codes cannot be used before 6 May 1990.

To find out what the new code will be from 6 May 1990, you can either look at the tables published in the latest (1989) edition of your local *Phone Book*, or else telephone (0800) 800 873, between 9 am and 7 pm, seven days a week. This call will be free.

The above codes relate to calls from *outside* London only. If you are calling from within the London telephone area (i.e. if you do not need to use the (01) prefix at present), you should continue to dial in exactly the same way after 6 May 1990 as before. There will be no change to the last seven digits of any London phone numbers.

Albany Video
The Albany, Douglas Way, London SE8 4AG, tel. (01) 692 0231

Avert Young People and Aids Project
Bristol Polytechnic, Department of Education, Redland Hill, Bristol B56 6UZ, tel. (0272) 741 251

The B-Team (Resources For Boyswork)
Box B-Team, BCM London WC1N 3XX

Beaumont Society
BM Box 3084, London WC1V 6XX. Provides counselling for transvestites.

Black HIV/AIDS Workers Group
C/O Rev. Hong Tan, Health Education Officer, London Borough of Hillingdon, Barra Hill, Wood End Green Road, Hayes, Middlesex UB3 2SA, tel. (01) 848 8700

Blackliners
Tel. (01) 673 1695. Advice and counselling for black people on HIV/AIDS.

Body Positive
BM AIDS, London WC1N 3XX. Help for those who are diagnosed HIV positive.

Boulton-Hawker Films Ltd
Hadleigh, Ipswich, Suffolk, IP7 5BG

Brook Advisory Centres
153A East Street, London SE17 2SD

Brothers Programme
c/o David Findlay, 207 Waller Road, Telegraph Hill, London
SE14 5LX. Courses for men on exploring the nature of
masculinity.

Childline
Tel. 0800 1111. Helpline for young people who are or have
been sexually abused. Also have a comprehensive list of local
agencies which offer services to survivors and abusers.

City and Hackney Young People's Project
St Leonard's Hospital, Nuttal Street, London N1 5LZ. Works
with young people on prevention of pregnancy and sex
education.

Concord Films Council
201 Felixtowe Road, Ipswich, Suffolk IP3 9 BJ

Everyman Publications
320 Commercial Way, London SE15 1QN. Publisher of
'Working with Men' newsletter.

Family Planning Association Education Unit (and bookshop)
27–35 Mortimer Street, London W1N 7RJ, tel. (01) 636 7866

Gracewell Clinic
81 Walkers Heath Road, Kings Norton, Birmingham B38 0AN,
tel. (021) 433 3888. Treatment for sex offenders including child
abusers.

Guild Sound and Vision
6 Royce Road, Peterborough PE1 5YB

Health Education Authority (HEA)
Hamilton House, Mabledon Place, London WC1H 9TX, tel. (01)
631 1930

HIV/AIDS Education and Young People Project
HIV/AIDS Research Unit, Christ Church College, North Holmes
Road, Canterbury, Kent CT1 1QU, tel. (0227) 762444

Incest Crisis Line
Tel. (01) 890 4732/422 5100. Advice for those who have been abused.

International Planned Parenthood Federation
Regents College, Inner Circle, Regents Park, London NW1 4NS, tel. (01) 486 0741. Has a library of books and films/videos.

London Lesbian and Gay Switchboard
BM Switchboard, London WC1N 3XX, tel. (01) 837 7324. Offers local and national information, advice and support on all aspects of gay men's and lesbians' lives, including HIV/AIDS.

Mens Therapy Centre
Tel. (01) 542 5059. Refers enquirers on to individual therapists who work with men.

MOVE – Men Overcoming Violence
1 Mark Lane, Bristol BS1 4XR, tel. (0272) 277301. Offers counselling to male sexual abuse survivors. Also will help men dealing with violence and will talk to abusers.

NAHAW (Network – the Association of HIV/AIDS Workers)
PO Box 1328, London W5 2BH. Provides support and information for HIV and AIDS workers.

National Audio-Visual Aids Library
The George Building, Normal College, Bangor, Gwynedd LL57 2PZ, tel. (0248) 370144

National Youth Bureau
17–23 Albion Street, Leicester LE1 66D, tel. (0533) 471200

North London Line
Tel. (01) 359 2884. Offers counselling and groups for young lesbians and gay men. Also provides support, information and counselling for young gay or bisexual men who have been abused or raped.

The Other Cinema
79 Wardour Street, London W1V 3TH, tel. (01) 734 8508/9

PACE (Project for Advice, Counselling and Education)
c/o London Lesbian and Gay Centre, 67–69 Cowcross Street, London EC1M 6BP, tel. (01) 251 2689

Relate (formerly the National Marriage Guidance Council) Herbert Gray College, Little Church Street, Rugby, Warwickshire, tel. (0788) 73241. Offers counselling to couples or single people. Ring for the address of your nearest branch.

Sex Education Forum
c/o The National Children's Bureau, 8 Wakely Street, London EC1V 9QE. A forum for organisations concerned with sex education.

Scottish AIDS Monitor
PO Box 169, Edinburgh EH1 3UU, tel. (031) 558 1167

SCODA (The Standing Conference On Drug Abuse)
1 Hatton Place, London EC1N 8ND, tel. (01) 430 2341

Shakti
Tel. (01) 993 9001 (evenings after 9.00pm and weekends, ask for Shivananda). A befriending service for Asian men and women who are homosexual, lesbian or bisexual.

Spectrum
7 Endymion Road, London N4 1EE, tel. (01) 341 2277/348 0196. Runs courses on sexuality for men and women and also the Spectrum Incest Intervention Project offering counselling to both incest survivors and perpetrators.

SPOD (Assoication to Aid the Sexual and Personal Relationships of People with a Disability)
286 Camden Road, London N7 0BJ, tel. (01) 607 8851

Survivors
Tel. (01) 833 3737 (daily, except Saturday 7–10 pm). For men, gay and straight, who have been raped.

Terence Higgins Trust
BM AIDS, London WC1N 3XX, helpline tel. (01) 242 1010, office (01) 831 0330. The major campaigning and support organisation on issues to do with HIV/AIDS.

Welsh AIDS Campaign
PO Box 348, Cardiff CF1 4XL, tel: (0222) 223443

Women's Health Information Centre
52–54 Featherstone Street, London EC1Y 8RT, tel. (01) 251 6589

Index

Other titles in the **Survival Handbooks** series:

Shirley Cooklin
From Arrest to Release: The Inside/Outside Survival Guide

Sandra Horley
Love and Pain: A Survival Handbook for Women

Tony Lake and Fran Acheson
Room to Listen, Room to Talk: A Beginner's Guide to Analysis, Therapy and Counselling

Jacquelynn Luben
Cot Deaths: Coping with Sudden Infant Death Syndrome

For further details, please write to the sales manager, Bedford Square Press, London WC1B 3HU

The Voluntary Agencies Directory

The Social Activists' Bible

NCVO's directory of voluntary agencies is the standard reference work for anyone who cares about helping the community.
It lists nearly 2,000 leading voluntary agencies, ranging from
small, specialist self-help groups to long-established national
charities. It gives concise, up-to-date descriptions of their aims
and activities, with details of

charitable status	local branches
volunteer participation	membership
trading activities	staffing

A list of useful addresses includes professional and public
advisory bodies concerned with voluntary action; a classified
index and quick reference list of acronyms and abbreviations
give easy access to entries.

There is extensive coverage of new groups concerned with
women's issues, minority rights, self-help, community development and leisure activities, environment and conservation,
campaigning and consumer affairs.

Voluntary agencies play an important part in making the world
a better place to live in. This NCVO directory is the essential
guide to their work.

'If you buy only one directory of voluntary agencies, buy this
one and buy it every year.' *Health Libraries Review*

'an essential working tool' *Environment Now*

The Health Directory
Compiled for the 'Thames Help' programme by Fiona Macdonald

In association with the College of Health and the Patients Association

A new edition of the former *Health Help* volume, first published by Bedford Square Press in 1987, the 1990/91 edition lists around 1,000 organisations set up to help patients and their families with many common (and not so common) health problems. They range from established national bodies such as the Red Cross and the NSPCC, to self-help groups dealing with a particular disorder.

Symbols are used to indicate when an organisation is a registered charity, has branches or local groups, welcomes volunteers or produces publications. The directory also includes organisations dealing with complementary medicine, ethnic minorities and general sources of help. The entries are listed alphabetically and in a comprehensive index by subject area.

The Parents' Directory
Compiled by Fiona Macdonald
Foreword by Esther Rantzen

'Whatever the problem . . . you only need spend a few minutes glancing through the pages of *The Parents' Directory* to see what an astonishing variety of voluntary bodies there are for parents to turn to . . . an excellent and comprehensive map.'
Esther Rantzen

The Parents' Directory lists around 800 voluntary organisations which are able to give help, advice and information to parents on a wide range of topics. The information is presented in easily accessible form under the headings Education, Family Welfare, Handicap, Health and Leisure, with each entry giving details of aims and objects, contact names and telephone. Symbols are used to give additional information in the same manner as that outlined for the *Health Directory*.

Forthcoming

The Women's Directory
Compiled by Fiona Macdonald

The Women's Directory will enable women who wish to make contact with others – whether for social, cultural, sporting, charitable, self-help or political purposes – to locate and identify suitable groups and organisations. It refers women to appropriate 'umbrella' bodies, whether voluntary, local-government-based or state funded, and gives other sources of information about women's activities, including relevant magazines and journals, publishers and bookshops. Presented in an accessible, simple-to-follow format, with symbols used to give additional information in the same manner as that outlined for *The Health Directory*.